THE LAW OF DAMAGES

The Law of Damages

by
Stewart Dunn
B.Sc., A.R.I.C.S., LL.B., Barrister.

NEWCASTLE UPON TYNE
Net Law Books
1999

To purchase copies of this book contact:
http://www.netlaw.freeserve.co.uk
Fax: (0191) 2580520 (UK)

First published 1999

ISBN 0 9529252 1 4

Printed in Great Britain by
Antony Rowe Ltd
Bumper's Farm
Chippenham,
Wiltshire SN14 6LH
Tel: (01249) 659705

CONTENTS

Table of Cases

Table of Statutes

Chapter 1

INTRODUCTION

a. The underlying principle

1.1 **Definition.** 'Damages' is the sum claimed or awarded in 'compensation' for 'damage,' 'loss' or 'injury'[1] caused by another's breach of duty.[2]

1.2 **The underlying principle.** The following leading statements of principle form the starting point in all actions for damages. The leading statement of principle in contract is that:

> "...where a party sustains a loss by reason of a breach of contract, he is, so far as money can do it, to be placed in the same situation with regard to damages as if the contract had been performed."[3]

---

[1] 'Damage,' 'loss,' 'injury' and the like are synonymous terms which refer to the 'effects' or 'consequences' of a breach of duty. The claimant is compensated in money regardless of whether the loss consists of financial loss, damage to property, personal injury, injury to reputation or some other type of loss.

[2] 'Duty' is used in a wide context so as to include a duty in contract and a duty in tort ('delict' in Scotland). Other remedies (outwith the scope of this book) may be available in respect of the same breach of duty, either in addition to or in the alternative to damages. For example, an injunction or specific performance order ('interdict' or 'specific implement' in Scotland) might be available to prevent the continuance of a breach of duty.

[3] Parke B in Robinson v Harman (1848)1 Ex. 850, 855/Dunlop v Higgins (1848) 6 Bell 195 at 211. This was described as the "underlying rule of the common law" by Lord Pearce in Koufos v Czarnikow Ltd (The Heron

In tort/delict the leading statement of principle is that:

> "...in settling the sum of money to be given for reparation of damages you should as nearly as possible get that sum of money which will put the party who has been injured, or who has suffered, in the same position as he would have been in if he had not sustained the wrong for which he is now getting his compensation or reparation."[4]

1.3   Analysis of the foregoing statements of principle reveals that the 'underlying principle' or 'purpose of an award of damages' is the same whether the action is in contract or in tort/delict.[5] The principle may be stated in the following way:

II) [1969]1 AC 350; [1967] 3 All ER 686 at 710, HL and as the "governing purpose of damages" by Asquith LJ in Victoria Laundry v Newman Industries [1949] 2 KB 528 at 539, CA; [1949] 1 All ER 997 at 1002, CA.

[4] per Lord Blackburn in Livingstone v Rawyards Coal Co (1880) 5 App Cas 25 at 39.

[5] Both statements contemplate restoring the claimant (as nearly as possible/so far as money can do it) to the position he would have been in 'but for' the breach of duty. The point may be further illustrated by Lord Wright's statement of principle in Monarch Steamship Co Limited v Karlshamns Oljefabriker (A/B) [1949] AC 196, HL at p220; [1949]1 All ER 1 at 12 (note that "contract" has been replaced with "duty" in order to extend the principle to tort/delict):
> "… the broad general rule of the law of damages [is] that a party injured by the other party's breach of ~~contract~~ [duty] is entitled to such money compensation as will put him in the position in which he would have been but for the breach."

The claimant is entitled to such sum of money (A) as compensates him (=)[6] for the difference between (-) the position in which he finds himself (C)[7] and the position which he would have been in 'but for' the breach of duty (B)[8]; A=C-B.

1.4 **Non-recoverable loss.** 'Liability' is limited to acts/events and types/kinds of loss which were the 'foreseeable' consequence of the breach of duty. These matters are considered in chapters 4 and 5.

In addition, the claimant is under a 'duty to mitigate' his loss/the effect of the breach (chapter 4 part b). Loss which could have been avoided had he complied with this duty is not recoverable, again on grounds of 'foreseeability' (4.4).

---

[6] The purpose of damages is to 'compensate' the claimant, by putting him **"as nearly as possible"** (Livingstone v Rawyards Coal Co (1.2)) in the position he would have been in but for the breach. Consequently, when the principle/purpose of damages is referred to as being 'restitutio in integrum' ('putting the injured party back into his original position') it impliedly means restitutio in integrum **"so far as money can do it"** (Robinson v Harman above). The term resitutio in integrum is also used in the context of a claim for 'recission' of a contract: see, for example Lord Blackburn in Erlanger v New Sombrero Phosphate Co (1878) 3 App Cas 1218 at 1278, [1874-80] All ER Rep 271 at 285-286. When used in that context it has a precise legal meaning and it must be possible to restore the parties to their original positions, which might involve returning monies paid/property transferred, before the remedy will be granted. The remedy is not therefore granted if the particular acts of performance make restitutio in integrum impossible.

[7] As allegedly worsened by the breach of duty.

[8] '...as if the contract had been performed,'/'...had he not sustained the wrong..'/'had the tort/delict not been committed.'

b. What the claimant must prove

Fig 1.1:What the Claimant must prove to be entitled to an award of damages

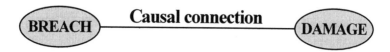

1.5 **What the claimant must prove.** In order to be entitled to an award of damages the claimant must prove the following:

1. The existence of a contract alternatively, if the action is in tort/delict, matters such as the status and relationship of the parties;
2. That the other party owed him a 'duty';[9]
3. 'Breach of duty';[10]
4. 'Causation': That the breach caused damage (causal connection between breach and damage);
5. That some injury/harm has been incurred and the

---

[9] For a common law claim in contract this would involve establishing that there were express and/or implied terms of the contract. In the case of a contractual claim the injured party would seek to rely on one or more of the 'specified' or 'relevant' or 'compensation' events listed in the clause dealing with claims for compensation. In tort/delict the claimant would be required to prove the existence of some common law or statutory duty owed to the claimant.

[10] This would entail proving breach of an express/implied term or, in the case of an 'express' claim (1.8), that one or more of the specified/relevant/compensation events expressed in the contract had occurred. If the action is founded in the tort/delict of negligence, the claimant must prove the things which the wrongdoer did which he ought not to have done and/or the things which he failed to do.

'amount'/'quantum' thereof (6.4).

1.6 'Fault,' 'liability' and 'extent of liability' distinguished.
The first 3 matters in 1.5 must be proved in order to establish
'fault.'[11] 'Breach of duty' = fault/negligence. Fault +
'causation' (chapter 2) = 'liability.'

Issues of 'foreseeability' (chapters 4 and 5) and issues as
to the 'amount'/'quantum' of damage (chapter 6) are
concerned with the 'extent of' a wrongdoer's liability.
Apportionment of liability (chapter 3), which is also
concerned with 'extent of' liability, is necessary where
damage is caused by the fault of more than one party.

c. Types of Remedy

1.7 Summary of potential remedies. The 'remedies' or 'causes
of action' which are relevant here include:
1. An action for damages for breach of contract at common
   law.
2. An action for compensation/damages pursuant to an
   express term dealing with recovery of compensation
   (referred to herein as an 'express' claim).
3. An action for damages for breach of a duty of care
   imposed by law (an action in tort/delict).

**1.8 Concurrent remedies in contract: 'express' claims and
'common law' claims.** A cause of action arises at common
law if there has been a breach of an express or implied term of
the contract. In addition, a contract may contain an express
provision which entitles the claimant to make a claim for
damages/recovery of compensation on the occurrence of some

---

[11] The law in relation to these 3 matters is out with the scope of this work.

'event' specified in the contract.'[12] If the 'event' in question would also amount to a breach of contract at common law then it could give rise to a 'concurrent cause of action' which would allow the claimant to pursue the claim on 'alternative' grounds.

The right to claim damages for breach of contract at common law exists independently of the 'express' right unless it has been expressly (or perhaps impliedly) modified or excluded by the wording of the contract. This depends on the intention of the parties/is a matter of construction of the particular contract."[13] Where there is an express provision in the contract for recovery of compensation ordinary common law damage principles (as discussed in Chapter 3) will apply to the assessment of the claimants entitlement unless the wording of contract indicates a contrary intention.[14]

1.9   Liquidated damages provisions. A contract may contain a 'liquidated damages' provision, that is one which stipulates an amount of money to be paid on the occurrence of a particular

---

[12] Examples include clause 26 of JCT 80 Standard Form of Building Contract and clauses 60-65 of the Engineering and Construction Contract.

[13] JCT 63 and 80 leave no room for doubt. See eg clause 26.6 of JCT 80 which expressly preserves the Contractor's common law rights. The effect of the co-existence of the two causes of action under JCT 63 was considered by Vinelott J in London Borough of Merton v Stanley Hugh Leach (1985) 32 BLR 51 at 108.

[14] If, for example, the contract allowed for recovery of 'additional costs incurred' then loss of profits (ordinarily recoverable in a common law claim) would not be recoverable. Under the Institution of Civil Engineers standard forms (ICE 5th/6th editions) loss of profits are not recoverable in relation to certain specified events.

breach of contract by one of the parties.[15] To be enforceable, the amount stipulated must be 'a genuine pre-estimate'[16] of the loss attributable to the breach in contemplation at the time of the pre-assessment.

If the amount stipulated is a 'genuine pre-estimate,' then the parties are bound by it/the assessment will be upheld. If the amount is not a 'genuine pre-estimate' it is deemed to be a 'penalty'/unenforceable and the injured party is entitled to recover the amount which he would have recovered if the correct principles had been applied in making the assessment, that is the amount of his 'common law' entitlement.[17] In effect the court substitutes its own assessment of damages which is the course of action it would take in an ordinary case if rejecting the basis of assessment advanced by the claimant in a claim for damages (6.7).

1.10 Whether a particular sum is a penalty or genuine pre-estimate is a question of construction to be decided at the date of the contract rather than at the date of the breach.[18] In deciding this issue the courts have indicated a reluctance to depart from the

---

[15] Damages which have not been assessed are said to be 'unliquidated' or 'at large.' Liquidated damages provisions are commonly found in respect of failure to complete a construction contract on time or failure to maintain payments under a contract of hire.

[16] Per Lord Robertson in Clydebank Engineering and Shipbuilding Co., Ltd. v. Castaneda [1905] AC 6 at p 19.

[17] Craig v M'Beath (1863) 1 M 1020; Cooden Engineering Co Ltd v Stanford [1953] 1 QB 86, [1952] 2 All ER 915; Bridge v Campbell Discount Co Ltd [1962] AC 600, [1962] 1 All ER 385; Jobson v Johnson [1989] 1 All ER 613, CA.

[18] Dunlop Pneumatic Tyre Co Ltd v New Garage and Motor Co Ltd [1915] AC 79 at 86–87 per Lord Dunedin.

amount stipulated in the contract.[19] If the stipulated sum is 'extravagantly greater than' or 'out of proportion' with any amount foreseeable as a result of the breach then it "... would give rise to the prima facie inference that the sum stipulated was a penalty."[20] The issue is analogous to the one which arises on an appeal as to the assessment of damages (6.27-8). The difference is that in the latter situation the court is reluctant to overturn a decision on a matter of fact rather than depart from/interfere with freedom of contract.

1.11 A particular feature of liquidated damages provisions is that, generally, only the total amount payable is inserted in the contract. It is only the party making the assessment, therefore, who knows how the amount was calculated. It would be undesirable for such a provision to be contractually binding since the party making the assessment would in effect be relieved of the burden of proof (6.4-6). On the present state of the law, if the party in breach wishes to have particulars of the claim he must challenge/dispute the amount stated in the

---

[19] The reason for this is a reluctance to interfere with freedom of contract and the belief that there are 'benefits' to the parties in reaching a binding agreement as to the amount of damages at the outset. Agreement in advance is thought to be advantageous in that the party in breach would know at the outset what its liability will be in the event of a breach of contract: see for example Robophone Facilities Ltd v Blank [1966] 1 WLR 1428, CA and Philips Hong Kong Ltd v The Attorney General of Hong Kong (1993) 61 BLR 41, PC. The apparent benefits are however questionable (1.11).

[20] Lord Diplock in Robophone Facilities Ltd v Blank [1966] 1 WLR 1428, CA at p1447; [1966] 3 All ER 128 at 143. See also Philips Hong Kong Ltd v The Attorney General of Hong Kong (1993) 61 BLR 41, PC.

contract.[21] The party in breach is then placed in the difficult position of an appellant on an assessment of damages when no burden of proof has been discharged by the other party.

The logical conclusion is that the mere insertion of a figure/figures as 'liquidated damages' amounts to a meaningless statement which is of no contractual effect. The claimant would therefore bear the burden of proof as he would do in an ordinary situation.

1.12 Concurrent remedies in contract and in tort/delict. If there is an implied term that one party will exercise reasonable care and skill in performance of a contract then, as a result of the proximity of the relationship between the parties, there is also likely to be a concurrent and identical duty of care in tort/delict. In such circumstances the claimant is free to pursue the remedy in tort/delict if he considers it to be to his advantage to do so.[22] The express wording of the contract is, however, important since the parties are, generally, free to modify or exclude common law rights.

---

[21] It would in ordinary circumstances be a sensible course of action to ask for 'appropriate' (6.4.-6) particulars of an unproven claim.

[22] Henderson v Merrett Syndicates Ltd, Hallam-Eames v Merrett Syndicates Ltd, Hughes v Merrett Syndicates Ltd, Arbuthnott v Feltrim Underwriting Agencies Ltd, Deeny v Gooda Walker Ltd (in *liq)* [1995] 2 AC 145; [1994] 3 All ER 506, HL. The actions in this case involved inter alia allegations of negligent advice given by underwriting agents to Lloyds names. The relevance of the claim to a right to sue in tort was that one of the causes of action was out with the contractual limitation period.

Chapter 2

CAUSATION

a. Introduction

2.1 **Definition.** In the words of Lord Wright:

> "Causation is a mental concept, generally based on inference or induction from uniformity of sequence as between two events that there is a causal connexion between them ..."[1]

2.2 **Issue of fact.** Causation is an issue of fact in respect of which there can be no rigid rule or test. Whether there is a causal connection between a particular factor and damage is something which must be ascertained by the standard of common sense of the ordinary man.[2]

2.3 **Causation and 'liability' distinguished.** In order to establish 'liability' it is necessary to prove that a causative factor was also a 'breach of duty'/'fault.' 'Fault' + 'causation' = 'liability' (1.6). This chapter is concerned solely with the issue of causation as a matter of fact (figure 2.1). The type of causal

---

[1] Monarch Steamship Co Limited v Karlshamns Oljefabriker (A/B) [1949] AC 196, HL at p229.

[2] Yorkshire Dale Steamship Co Ltd v Minister of War Transport, The Coxwold [1942] AC 691; [1942] 2 All ER 6, HL. In the Monarch Steamship case (2.1/4.19) Lord Wright said (at p229) that:
> "The common law ...is not concerned with philosophic speculation, but is only concerned with ordinary everyday life and thoughts and expressions."

connection may, however, depend on whether certain parties owe concurrent duties to the claimant (2.26)

Fig 2.1: The issue - is there a causal connection?

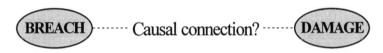

2.4 **Burden and standard of proof.** It is for the claimant to prove (the burden), on the balance of probabilities (the standard), that there is a causal connection between breach and damage. The burden is discharged by adducing evidence which 'tends to show' or which leads to an inference that the breach caused damage.

2.5 **Construction contracts.** In a construction contract where delay and/or interruption has occurred, the contractor may have submitted a 'cause and effect' schedule in support of his claim for damages. In this context 'cause' means 'alleged cause, breach or relevant event.' 'Effect' means 'alleged damage or delay.' Whether causation can be inferred from the schedule alone will depend on the circumstances.[3] In a clear case, such as with a variation requiring a significant quantity of additional work, it may not be necessary to adduce further evidence and the only issue may be as to the amount of loss/damage, that is the 'extent of' the wrongdoer's liability.

---

[3] It will be necessary for the person being asked to make the inference to be aware, for example, of the effects of changes in design on the progress of the work. If this knowledge is not possessed then further professional advice should be sought.

In a situation of any complexity, however, it may be necessary to consider other types of evidence.[4]

2.6 **Starting point - the 'but for' test.** The claimant is entitled to be placed in the position he would have been in 'but for' the breach (1.2-3). It follows that if the claimant would have incurred the loss/have been in the same position in any event/irrespective of the factor under consideration, then that factor cannot have been causative of damage. The but for test serves to eliminate from the equation those factors which were not potentially causative and in a simple case it may be possible to resolve the issue of causation by application of this test alone.[5]

b. Potential causal scenarios

2.7 In many situations it will not be possible to resolve the issue by the 'but for' test alone. There will commonly be a number of potentially causative factors (figure 2.2) and in such circumstances there are a variety of causal scenarios which could arise. Whatever the scenario, it is helpful to remember that there can only be one 'cause' of a particular amount of damage.

---

[4] Other types of evidence include: programmes showing planned (ie 'but for') and actual progress, indicating when the breach or relevant event occurred; photographs indicating areas affected by delay/where progress could not be made; network analysis and expert evidence; oral evidence of the parties.

[5] Application of the 'but for' test in relation to 'liability for consequential acts and events' is considered at 4.1 and 4.17.

Fig 2.2: Typical situation

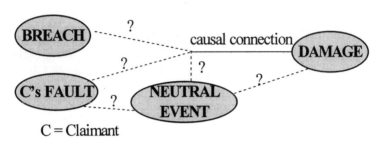

C = Claimant

2.8   Potential Scenarios. The following possibilities arise out of the situation envisaged by figure 2.2:

1. Only one factor is causative (figure 1.1).

2. 2 or more causes of separate/distinct damage (figure 2.3). This scenario also applies if the loss is a 'global'/cumulative one (figure 6.1).[6] Alternatively there could be a second/subsequent cause of 'further' damage which breaks the 'chain of causation' (a 'new and independent' cause: figure 4.2).[7]

3. 2 or more 'concurrent' causes of the 'same' or 'overlapping' amount of damage (figures 2.4, 2.5 and 2.6).

4. Damage caused by the combined effect of two or more factors, referred to herein as a 'composite'/'compound'

---

[6] 'Apportionment of damage' may be necessary in the case of a global loss (figure 6.3).

[7] Chapter 4 also deals with the situation in which damage is caused by the claimant's 'failure to mitigate' (chapter 4 part b).

cause (figures 2.7, 2.8, 2.9 and 2.10).[8]

5. 'Chain of causation.' This situation arises if one factor is a consequence of another (figure 2.9 and 4.1).

Fig 2.3: Causes of separate/distinct damage

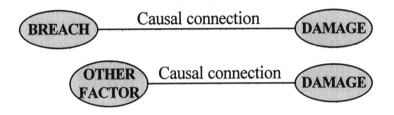

c. 'Concurrent' causes

2.9 **Introduction.** If two factors, when considered in isolation, would each have caused the same type/kind of damage of the same or overlapping amount then they may be referred to as 'concurrent' causes of that damage. In such a situation the 'first in time' to cause 'prospective' damage[9] of the particular

---

[8] The distinction between 'cumulative' damage caused by a several causative of factors and 'one and indivisible' damage caused by the combined effect of several factors is considered at 2.22.

[9] A 'prospective,' that is 'expected' or 'likely' loss may not be recoverable if a subsequent 'supervening' cause/event prevents the loss from being incurred (2.17-20).

type/kind is the causative factor (figures 2.4 and 2.5).[10,11]

If it is not possible to eliminate concurrent causes/attribute whole blame to one factor by application of the 'first in time' rule one alternative would be to apportion liability (chapter 3).

Fig 2.4: Concurrent causes of the same damage

2.10 **Application of the 'first in time' rule.** In the road accident case of *Performance Cars Ltd v Abraham*,[12] A collided with B and, thereafter on a different occasion, C also collided with B (figure 2.4). Each collision independently required the same

---

[10] When applying the but for test to a particular factor, therefore, only those factors which occur earlier in the chronology of events should be taken into account. In figure 2.4 it is only in relation to breach 2 that it could be said that the damage would have been incurred due to an earlier factor/'in any event'/'but for' the breach.

[11] The 'first in time rule' has not been applied in actions for defamation/libel. In such actions the claimant can recover damages in respect of the whole injury caused by a wrongdoer even though some of the damage was caused (concurrently) by another wrongdoer's previously committed act of defamation/libel: see for example *Dingle v Associated Newspapers Ltd* [1961] 2 QB 162 at 189, [1961] 1 All ER 897 at 916.

[12] [1962] 1 QB 33; [1961] 3 WLR 749; [1961] 3 All ER 413, CA.

part of B's vehicle to be resprayed but only A was liable. C's fault was not a causative factor since the repairs would have been required in any event/but for the fault on his part.

2.11 In The Haversham Grange,[13] a vessel was damaged in two successive collisions, each collision causing distinct (non-identical) physical damage (separate causes of separate damage: figure 2.3) and each rendering the vessel unseaworthy (concurrent causes of the same/overlapping damage). If carried out in isolation, the first collision repairs would have taken 22 days and the second collision repairs 6 days. Both sets of repairs were carried out concurrently in a period of 22 days. The owners of the Haversham Grange were responsible for the second collision (and therefore the costs of repairing the distinct physical damage attributable thereto) but were not liable for the loss of profits incurred while the ship was laid up during the repairs, since the 6 days loss of profit (the 'same'/'overlapping' damage) was concurrently caused by/attributable to the earlier collision (figure 2.5).[14]

---

[13] [1905] P 307.

[14] Note that the owners of the Haversham Grange were not liable for the 6 days loss of profit due to application of the 'first in time' rule and not because the earlier collision was the 'dominant'/greater cause (2.15). A similar situation arose in The Carslogie (2.20).

Fig 2.5 Concurrent causes of the same damage
(Loss of profits: The Haversham Grange)

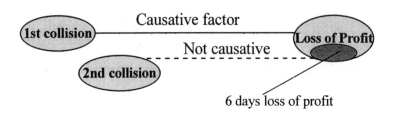

2.12 In Baker v Willoughby[15] the claimant suffered a severe leg injury in a road accident. As a result of a subsequent shooting, the leg had to be amputated. The whole loss was nevertheless attributable to the initial injury since the subsequent factor was regarded as being a cause of identical injury. Lord Reid said that the damages recoverable from the defendant should not be reduced if "the later injuries merely become a concurrent cause of the disabilities caused by the injury inflicted by the defendant."[16]

2.13 Problems concerning concurrent causes of damage/delay are commonly encountered in construction contracts. The contractor may, for example, have failed to achieve completion by the contractual date due to poor quality workmanship or as a result of slow progress. If the Architect issues instructions requiring additional work which would, if considered in isolation, also have delayed completion (a

---

[15] [1970] AC 467; [1969] 3 All ER 1528, HL.

[16] [1970] AC 467 (HL) at 494.

concurrent cause of the delay) the question arises as to whether the contractor is entitled to an extension of time or damages. Assuming no further delay is caused in carrying out the additional work then, applying the principles set out above, the contractor would have no entitlement. The problem was considered by Colman J in Balfour Beatty Building Ltd v Chestermount Properties Ltd,[17] a case which was concerned with clause 25 of the JCT 80 standard form of building contract, Private edition with Approximate Quantities. In relation to the situation in which a contractor is already in delay at the time of the issue of the instructions his Lordship said:

> "If the variation works can reasonably be conducted simultaneously with the original works without interfering with their progress and are unlikely to prolong practical completion, the architect might properly conclude that no extension of time was justified. He would therefore leave the completion date where it was. That would leave the contractor to pay liquidated damages for the amount of time by which he had exceeded the original period of time for completion."

2.14 Subsequent factor causes further damage. If a subsequent factor is a cause of further, non-identical damage, the

---

[17] (1993), 62 BLR 1 at 31.

subsequent wrongdoer is liable for that further damage.[18]

2.15 Subsequent damage is greater than the whole of/subsumes the initial damage. Any damage caused by the initial factor remains the liability of the initial wrongdoer even if the damage attributable to the subsequent factor would independently have 'subsumed' or caused greater damage than whole of the (same) damage attributable to the earlier factor (figure 2.6).[19] It is the 'first in time' rule rather than the 'dominant cause theory' or 'dominant test' which applies.

Fig 2.6: The 'dominant test' is not the correct one

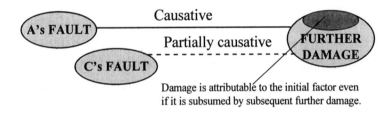

Damage is attributable to the initial factor even if it is subsumed by subsequent further damage.

---

[18] In The Haversham Grange (2.11), for example, the owners of the Haversham Grange were liable for the cost of carrying out the necessary repairs/the distinct physical damage.

[19] In The Haversham Grange (2.11) therefore, the owners of the Haversham Grange would have been liable for the 6 days loss of profit if they had caused the first collision and the subsequent wrongdoer would have been liable for the remaining 16 days (illustrated by figure 2.6).

Note that the 'dominant' cause does not 'prevent' the earlier damage from being incurred as in the situation considered at 2.17-20. The dominant factor may be described as an 'independent' but not 'supervening' factor/event.

2.16 In Fairweather (H) & Co Ltd v London Borough of Wandsworth,[20] the arbitrator found that the whole of an 81 week delay had been caused by strikes and combination of workmen, a 'neutral event'[21] under the contract. The contractor, in order to recover part of his loss, sought to argue that part of the extension of time should be reallocated to the provision relating to architect's instructions (a concurrent cause of delay). The arbitrator had awarded the entire extension pursuant to the strike on the ground that it was the greater/'dominant' delay. In relation to this approach, His Honour Judge Fox-Andrews QC said that:

> ".....an architect and in his turn an arbitrator has the task of allocating, when the facts require it, the extension of time to the various heads. I do not consider that the dominant test is correct."[22]

The necessary findings of fact were matters for the arbitrator to decide. On the assumption however, that the relevant instructions were the first in time to cause prospective delay and/or damage, then an appropriate amount of the delay/damage should have been allocated to the relevant instructions.

---

[20] (1987) 39 BLR 106. The case concerned an action under JCT 1963, Local Authorities edition, With Quantities.

[21] That is, an event in respect of which an extension of time may be granted but no direct loss and/or expense is recoverable.

[22] (1987), QBD 39 BLR 106 at 120.

d. 'Supervening' causes

2.17 Effect of 'supervening' causes/events on recovery of 'prospective' loss. The general rule is that a party can recover 'prospective,' that is 'expected' or 'likely' future loss where breach of duty and causation have been proved. When a 'prospective' loss is awarded, however, it is based on the assumption that the claimant will in fact incur the loss claimed. Such loss will not, therefore, be recoverable if a 'supervening' factor has occurred between the date of the breach and the date of the trial of the action to prevent all or part of the loss from being incurred.[23] The general rule is that:

> "...when damages which would be otherwise prospective come to be assessed, facts which have actually happened may be taken into account,..."[24]

---

[23] A 'concurrent' cause may be distinguished in that it causes the same or overlapping damage of the same type/kind. It does not prevent the loss from being incurred. Similarly, 'dominant' causes (2.15-16) merely cause 'greater' loss of the same type/kind.

A 'supervening' factor must be an 'independent' factor/event and not a 'consequential' factor/event. If the factor/event is a 'consequence' of the initial wrong then the wrongdoer may be liable for that consequence and in respect of any additional damage attributable thereto (Chapter 4).

[24] per Scrutton LJ in The Kingsway [1918] P. 344 at 362. Such a situation could arise in a construction contract, for example, if the building was destroyed before delay caused by the contractor results in actual loss to the employer. If the completion date had already passed, however, at the time the building was destroyed the contractor would be liable for the damage caused up to that point: See, for example, Associated Portland Cement v Houlder Brothers & Co (1917) 86 LJKB 1495.

2.18 In The Glenfinlas,[25] the vessel had been damaged and was in need of repair. Before the repairs could be carried out, however, she was lost at sea (the independent and supervening event). The loss of profits which would have been incurred whilst repairs were being carried out (the 'prospective' loss) could no longer be recovered since the repairs never could or would have been done and the vessel was no longer capable of profitable employment. The cost of the repairs was, however, recoverable since, at the time of sinking, the ship was of less value to the owners and the cost of repairs represented the 'diminution in value' of the vessel. Diminution in value is not, therefore, a head of claim which is to be regarded as prospective loss.

2.19 The Glenfinlas was applied in Beoco Ltd v Alfa Laval Co Ltd and Another.[26] In that case the supplier of a defective heat exchanger was not liable under the contract for 'hypothetical' loss of profits (the prospective loss) when the exchanger had exploded before the repairs could be carried out. The supplier was, however, liable for the cost of repair which represented its diminution in value.[27]

---

[25] [1918] P 363n, [1918-19] All ER Rep 365n.

[26] [1994] 4 All ER 464; (1993) 66 BLR 1, CA.

[27] "...what was damaged in the explosion was not a sound heat exchanger with 18 years' life in it, but a defective one with much less." per Stuart-Smith LJ [1994] 4 All ER 464 (CA) at 473.

2.20 In The Carslogie,[28] the plaintiff's vessel was damaged in a collision which was the fault of the Carslogie. Temporary repairs (due to war restrictions) were carried out making her seaworthy and fit to work. On the way to the port where amongst other things permanent repairs were to be carried out, she was rendered unseaworthy and in need of immediate repair due to heavy weather damage.[29] During her time in dry dock (50 days) the repairs due to the collision, additional engine repairs[30] and the heavy weather repairs were all done concurrently. It was agreed that 10 days out of the 50 should be allocated to the repair of the collision damage and that 30 days would have been required for the heavy weather damage. It was held that the claimant could not recover for a lost opportunity of earning profits during the 10 day period. The reason for this was that the vessel was 'unseaworthy,' due to the heavy weather damage and not therefore a 'profit-earning

---

[28] Carslogie Steamship Co Ltd v Royal Norwegian Government, The Carslogie [1952] AC 292, HL; [1952] 1 All ER 20, HL.

[29] "The heavy weather damage was not in any sense a consequence of the collision, and must be treated as a supervening event occurring in the course of a normal voyage,....." per Viscount Jowitt [1952] 1 All ER 20, HL at 22. If the heavy weather damage had been a consequence of the collision the plaintiff may have been entitled to recover the full 30 days loss of profits from the owners of the Carslogie (chapter 4).

[30] The fact that the plaintiff had also taken the opportunity to have some maintenance carried out at the same time as the collision repairs would not have prejudiced his claim against the defendants: for example, Ruabon Steamship Co. Ld. v The London Assurance [1900] AC 6. If however, such other maintenance or repairs had been required of necessity it may have been otherwise: Admiralty Commissioners v The Chekiang (Owners) [1926] AC 637, The Carslogie at [1952] AC 292 (HL) at 301-302.

machine' at the time the repairs were carried out. In other words the owners suffered 'no loss.'[31] Unseaworthiness therefore had the same effect as sinking the ship, such as in The Glenfinlas (2.18), would have had.

If the view is taken that loss of profits were in fact incurred then the heavy weather would have been a 'concurrent' cause of the loss (The Haversham Grange) rather than a 'supervening' factor which prevented it from being incurred (The Glenfinlas). On this view, applying the first in time rule, the owners of the Carslogie would be liable for 10 days loss of profits.[32]

e. 'Composite'/'compound' causes

2.21 Composite/compound causes generally. A composite/compound cause exists where 2 or more causative factors combine/converge to cause 'one and indivisible' damage (figure 2.7). The matter of composite causation was considered by Devlin LJ In Dingle v Associated Newspapers Ltd.[33] With reference to a situation in which a finding of composite causation would be appropriate, His Lordship said that:

---

[31] No loss of profits were in any event incurred due to existing unseaworthiness: per Lord Normand [1952] AC 292, HL at 301 and Lord Morton [1952] AC 292, HL at p315.

[32] For a case concerning supervening causes in the personal injury context see Jobling v Associated Dairies Ltd [1982] AC 794, HL; [1981] 2 All ER 752, HL.

[33] [1961] 2 QB 162, CA at 189; [1961] 1 All ER 897, CA at 916.

"It is essential for this purpose that the loss should be one and indivisible; whether it is so or not is a matter of fact and not a matter of law."

Fig 2.7: Composite cause (eg road accident)[34]

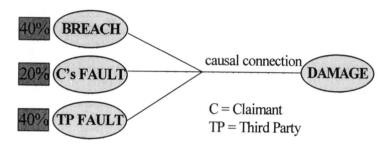

2.22 **'One and indivisible' loss and ' global' loss distinguished.** A 'one and indivisible' loss is caused by the 'combined' effect of 2 or more causative factors. A 'global' loss (figures 6.1 and 6.3) on the other hand is one which is caused by the 'cumulative' effect of 2 or more causative factors. In a 'global' loss situation the amount of loss caused by each factor is difficult to identify.[35] The loss in a 'global' loss

---

[34] Apportionment of 'liability' is considered in Chapter 3.

[35] The distinction was also considered by Mustill J in Thompson and others v Smiths Shiprepairers (North Shields) Ltd (6.24-26) at 907- 908. In distinguishing hearing loss sustained over a period of approximately thirty years from the type of situation envisaged by Devlin LJ His Lordship said that:

"This condition is not the direct product of a group of acts, not necessarily simultaneous, but all converging to bring about one occurrence of damage. Rather, it is the culmination of a progression,

situation may therefore be said to be 'one' and 'difficult/impracticable to divide' but not 'indivisible.' In one situation the problem is one of apportionment/division of liability and in the other the problem is one of apportionment/division of damage.[36]

2.23 Composite causes involving a 'latent'/existing breach. 2 factors may combine/converge to cause one and indivisible damage notwithstanding the fact that they have not occurred simultaneously. This possibility arises where a 'latent'/existing breach, which may not otherwise have been causative of damage,[37] combines/converges with a subsequent factor to cause (one and indivisible) damage.

---

the individual stages of which were each brought about by the separate acts of the persons sued, or (as the case may be) the separate non-faulty and faulty acts of the only defendant. In my judgment, the principle stated by Devlin LJ does not apply to this kind of case."

[36] The distinction so far as apportionment is concerned is considered at 3.3 and 6.20.

[37] The latent breach would not have been causative in the Smith Hogg case (2.24). In Government of Ceylon v Chandris (6.21-23) damage was caused to the cargo by the combined effect of the non-latent breach (inadequate fitting of the vessel) and the delay caused by the default of the charterer.

Fig 2.8: Composite cause involving a 'latent' or 'non-latent' breach

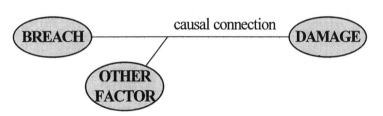

2.24 In Smith Hogg and Co Ltd v Black Sea & Baltic General Insurance Co Ltd,[38] unseaworthiness of a vessel (a latent breach attributable to the owners of the ship) coupled with the loading of cargo caused the vessel to list. She had to be abandoned and there was loss and damage to cargo due to water ingress. Liability was attributed to the unseaworthiness alone as the subsequent factor, although causative/essential for the occurrence of the damage, did not involve a breach of duty. There was therefore no 'fault' (1.6) on the part of the master in loading the ship.

2.25 **Composite causation in the case of consequential acts and events ('chain of causation').** If the claimant's actions or the occurrence of an event is 'a consequence of' an earlier factor/breach then a 'chain of causation' may come into existence (figure 2.9).[39] This is a special type of composite

---

[38] [1940] AC 997.

[39] In a chain of causation situation the initial factor is causative of the second factor *and* of any damage incurred: Viscount Haldane in The Metagama (4.5). The initial factor and the consequential act amount in

cause situation (chapter 4) in which, generally, only one party will be liable. Joint fault may be appropriate if the claimant[40] or a third party[41] is negligent in performing the consequential act.

Fig 2.9: Composite causation: breach followed by consequential act/event

f. Where the type of cause depends on the existence of concurrent duties.

2.26 **Composite causation arising from concurrent duties owed to the claimant.** In some situations the cause of damage may be known but the type of causal scenario may depend on which of a number of respondents owed (concurrent) duties to

---

effect to 1 causative factor.

[40] Examples include Sayers v Harlow Urban District Council (4.8/figure 4.3); The Calliope (4.9/figure 4.4). In The Wagon Mound (No1) there was potential joint liability (contributory negligence) on the part of the owners of the wharf (4.22-23).

[41] Burrows v March Gas & Coke Co (4.18) is a case in which a finding of joint fault could potentially have been made.

the claimant (figure 2.10).[42] In such cases the 'liability' issue depends on whether there was a 'duty' of care/fault rather than whether there was a 'causal connection' between breach and damage.[43]

Under a typical construction contract, for example, the architect acts as the agent of the employer. The architect is responsible for design of the work and the contractor is responsible for construction. If damage results from defective design an issue may arise as to whether the contractor should be jointly liable, based on an implied 'duty to warn' the architect of the design problem. On the other hand if the contractor does not construct the building according to the design the issue may be whether there was an implied duty on the part of the architect to supervise[44] or on the part of the local authority to inspect the work.

---

[42] The duties may arise from separate contracts which the claimant has entered into or from duties imposed by common law or statute in the case of tort/delict.

[43] 'Fault'/breach of duty + 'causation' = 'liability' (1.6).

[44] Since the architect acts as agent of the employer, there could be an assertion of joint fault/contributory negligence on the part of the employer if he was the claimant in the action (2.28-end, illustrated by the case of Barclays Bank plc v Fairclough Building Ltd and Others (2.32)).

Fig 2.10: Composite causation: latent/existing breach and a failure to act

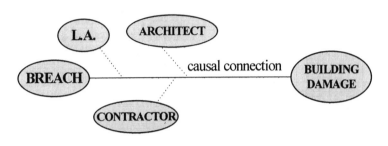

2.27 In Anns and others v London Borough of Merton,[45] for example, dwellings were damaged due to the fact that the foundations had not been constructed to the depth approved by the local authority. A breach of duty by the builder was causative of damage. In addition it was alleged by the claimants/occupiers that the local authority should be liable on the ground that they had failed to inspect the completed work.

2.28 Composite causation involving joint fault on the part of the claimant. Joint fault may arise in this context if, for example, the claimant is in breach of a 'duty to avoid loss/injury to himself.' This would generally give rise to a defence of 'contributory negligence' (chapter 3 part c).

2.29 Joint fault on the part of the claimant in contract. The duty on the part of the claimant to take reasonable care for his own safety/to avoid loss/injury to himself arises, as in other duty situations, at the point at which he ought to have foreseen that

---

[45] Anns and others v London Borough of Merton [1978] AC 728; [1977] 2 WLR 1024; [1977] 2 All ER 492, HL.

a want of care on his part could result in injury to himself.

Except in the case of the duty to avoid personal injury to himself,[46] the implication of a contractual term/duty to avoid loss arising from a breach by the other party would generally be inappropriate. This is due to the fact that it would probably conflict with the express terms/the intention of the parties.

2.30 A further reason is the 'rule of construction' that:

"....generally speaking, a man is entitled to act in the faith that the other party to a contract is carrying out his part of it properly."[47]

2.31 Implied terms/duties and the 'duty to mitigate' distinguished. No term/duty is generally implied due in part to the fact that breaches of contract are not generally 'foreseeable.' The conditions for the imposition of a duty to avoid loss do not therefore exist until, generally, a claimant is aware that the breach has occurred. At this point the law

---

[46] In the case of the duty to avoid personal injury, a claimant generally bears this duty notwithstanding the existence of a contract. A defence of contributory negligence would therefore be available, for example, in actions between employer and employee. Sayers v Harlow Urban District Council (4.8/figure4.3) is a case in which there was concurrent liability in contract/tort. The effect of the contract may, however, be such as to exclude a defence of contributory negligence: Barclays Bank plc v Fairclough Building Ltd and Others [1995] 1 All ER 279, CA.

[47] per Devlin J in Cia Naviera Maropan S/A v Bowaters Lloyd Pulp and Paper Mills Ltd [1955] 2 QB 68 at 77; [1954] 3 All ER 563 at 568, approved by the Privy Council in Reardon Smith Line Ltd and Australian Wheat Board [1956] AC 266 at 282; [1956] 1 All ER 456 at 46; applied in Barclays Bank plc v Fairclough Building Ltd and Others (2.32).

imposes a duty on all claimants (whether due to a breach of contract or breach of duty in tort/delict) which is referred to as the 'duty to mitigate'/avoid loss. This matter is considered at chapter 4 part c.

2.32 **Joint fault in construction contracts.** In Barclays Bank plc v Fairclough Building Ltd and Others[48] the bank employed a main contractor, under the JCT Intermediate Form of Contract 1984 edition, to carry out inter alia specialist cleaning of asbestos roofing. As a result of the method of cleaning adopted (high pressure water jet), water penetrated through the joints in the roofing and into the bank's premises. When the water dried, it left a high quantity of asbestos dust and prohibition notices were issued by the council requiring that work should cease. The bank claimed £4m in respect of the extensive remedial works which were required. In its defence, the contractor alleged contributory negligence on the part of the bank in failing, inter alia, to condemn the method of working or to prevent accidents or adverse affects on the health of its employees. On the facts of the case no term was to be implied such as would have given rise to a defence of contributory negligence under the Law Reform (Contributory Negligence) Act 1945 (3.9). In conclusion, Beldam LJ stated that:

> "...[Even if the 1945 Act did apply[49]], in the present case the nature of the contract and the obligation undertaken by the skilled contractor did not impose on

---

[48] (1994) 68 BLR 1; [1995] 1 All ER 279, CA.

[49] This issue is considered at 3.11.

the bank any duty in its own interest to prevent the contractor from committing the breaches of contract. To hold otherwise would, I consider, be equivalent to implying into the contract an obligation on the part of the bank inconsistent with the express terms agreed between the parties. The contract clearly laid down the extent of the obligations of the bank as architect and of the contractor. It was the contractor who was to provide appropriate supervision on site, not the architect."[50]

---

[50] [1995] 1 All ER 279, CA at 303; (1994) 68 BLR 1, CA at 21G-I.

Chapter 3

APPORTIONMENT OF LIABILITY

a. Introduction

3.1   Generally. Apportionment of liability is necessary if a specific amount of (one and indivisible) damage is caused by the convergence/combined effect of 2 or more causative factors, that is in a 'composite' cause (2.21-end) situation.[1] A causative factor must also amount to a breach of duty if liability is to be attached thereto.[2]

3.2   How liability is apportioned. Apportionment of liability (figure 2.7) involves an assessment of the 'relative fault/blameworthiness'[3] of each causative factor. In The

---

[1] Another situation in which apportionment of liability could be appropriate is considered at 2.9, that is in the case of concurrent causes if it is not practicable/possible to eliminate any of the concurrent factors by application of the 'first in time rule.'

[2] 'Liability' consists of 'fault' ('breach of duty') plus 'causation' (1.6). In Smith Hogg and Co Ltd v Black Sea & Baltic General Insurance Co Ltd (2.24), for example, no liability was attached to the second causative factor as it did not involve any fault/negligence/breach of duty.

[3] "When it is necessary for a court to ascribe liability in proportions to more than one person, it is well established that regard must be had not only to the causative potency of the acts or omissions of each of the parties, but to their relative blameworthiness:" Winn LJ in Brown and Another v Thompson [1968] All ER 708, CA.

Miraflores and The Abadesa[4] Lord Pearce said that:

> "To get a fair apportionment it is necessary to weigh the fault of each negligent party against that of the others."

3.3 **Distinction between 'apportionment of liability' and 'apportionment of damage.'**[5] Apportionment of damage is concerned with an assessment of the 'relative effect' of each causative factor (6.20) rather than the 'relative fault/blameworthiness' attributable thereto. The difference in the approach is due to the distinction in the nature of the loss incurred (2.22). In each case, however, the purpose of the exercise is the same, that is to assess the extent of the wrongdoer's liability for the total loss incurred.

3.4 **Apportionment of liability under statute.** A further distinction between apportionment of liability and apportionment of damage is that in the former situation apportionment is made pursuant to statute (3.8 and 3.9) whereas in the latter situation apportionment is made pursuant to a common law power.[6] In view of the similarities between

---

[4] The Miraflores and The Abadesa Owners of the Steam Tanker Miraflores v Owners of the Steam Tanker George Livanos and Others [1967] 1 AC 826, [1967] 2 WLR 806, [1967] 1 All ER 672, HL.

[5] This is also considered at 6.20.

[6] Prior to a statutory power to apportion liability, 'contributory negligence' would for example have been a complete defence. This point was considered in The Wagon Mound (No 2) (4.23).

the 2 situations[7] it could be argued that where apportionment of liability is appropriate this could/should also be made pursuant to a common law power.

3.5 **Procedure.** Ideally all issues, including apportionment of liability, should be dealt with in one action.[8] If the claimant does not join all wrongdoers, by joining them as co-defendants to the action, then any wrongdoer who is a defendant can join any of the other wrongdoers by way of third party proceedings in the same action.[9]

Alternatively, wrongdoer's may recover a contribution (3.8) by way of a separate action, after decree/judgement in the other action.

b. Apportionment of liability between joint wrongdoers

3.6 **Whole loss recoverable from any wrongdoer.** In Dingle v Associated Newspapers Ltd[10] Devlin LJ stated that the position in tort is that:

"Where injury has been done to the plaintiff and the

---

[7] Illustrated by The Calliope (4.9/figure 4.4) and Government of Ceylon v Chandris (6.21-23/figure 6.4).

[8] To arrive at the correct apportionment it is necessary to consider the relative fault of all parties (3.2). One action also avoids unnecessary duplication of time and costs. The court will not, however, take account of any possible negligence of a party who is not a party to the proceedings: Mayfield v Llwelleyn [1961] 1 WLR 119.

[9] In Scotland a 'defender' make a plea 'all parties not called' in his 'defences.'

[10] [1961] 2 QB 162 at 188-189; [1961] 1 All ER 897 at 916, CA.

injury is indivisible, any tortfeasor whose act has been a proximate cause of the injury must compensate for the whole of it.[11] As between the plaintiff and the defendant it is immaterial that there are others whose acts also have been a cause of the injury and it does not matter whether those others have or have not a good defence. These factors would be relevant in a claim between tortfeasors for contribution [(3.8)], but the plaintiff is not concerned with that; he can obtain judgment for total compensation from anyone whose act has been a cause of his injury:"[12]

3.7 In Thompson and others v Smiths Shiprepairers (North Shields) Ltd (6.24-26) Mustill J said (at p908) that:

"It is a pragmatic rule, designed to avoid the unjust conclusion that a plaintiff who cannot establish the precise degree to which the wrongful act has contributed to the loss must fail entirely for want of proof..."[13]

---

[11] This is the case if a wrongdoer is only 1% at fault.

[12] If the loss/injury was caused partly by the claimant's own negligence then the wrongdoer could raise a defence of 'contributory negligence' (3.9-end).

[13] The rule can cause injustice in that there may be causative factors which are not the fault of any party. In such a case an alternative approach could be to apply the rule which is applied when 'apportionment of damage' is being considered, namely that "the court should make the best estimate which it can, in the light of the evidence," (6.8) in this case of the 'relative fault/blameworthiness' of each causative factor.

Alternatively, one wrongdoer may not be able to obtain 'contribution' (3.8) from another if the other is unable to satisfy judgement. In such circumstances apportionment should perhaps also be considered. If other

3.8   Civil Liability (Contribution) Act 1978. In England and Wales, the right of one wrongdoer to recover an appropriate contribution from a person liable in respect of the same damage is derived from the Civil Liability (Contribution) Act 1978.[14]

s.1(1) provides that.

> "Subject to the following provisions of this section, any person liable in respect of any damage suffered by another person may recover contribution from any other person liable in respect of the same damage (whether jointly with him or otherwise)."[15]

Assessment of contribution is governed by s.2(1) of the Act which provides that:

> "......the amount of contribution recoverable from any person shall be such as may be found by the court to be just and equitable having regard to the extent of that person's responsibility for the damage in question."

---

wrongdoers are joined as parties to the action (3.5) liability can be apportioned by the court at the time of judgement.

[14] This Act does not apply in Scotland except para 1 schedule 1. In Scotland the relevant source is the Law Reform (Miscellaneous Provisions) (Scotland) Act 1940, s.3.

[15] There would appear to be no reason why the claimant could not be 'any other person liable...'

c. Apportionment when the claimant is jointly liable ('contributory negligence').

3.9   Apportionment under the Law Reform (Contributory Negligence) Act 1945.[16] If the claimant is under a 'duty to avoid loss/injury to himself'[17] and his loss/injury was caused by the combined effect of his own breach of duty/fault/negligence and a breach of duty by another party then the party defending the action can raise a defence of 'contributory negligence.'[18,19] If the defence is successful,

---

[16] The Act applies in England and Wales and in Scotland.

[17] As in the case of a 'duty to take reasonable care for his own safety:' dictum of Lord Atkin in Caswell v Powell Duffryn Associated Collieries Ltd [1940] AC 164; 161 LT 377; [1939] 3 All ER 730.

[18] An example of contributory negligence would be a passenger's failure to wear a seatbelt (figure 2.7). Cases involving contributory negligence include Sayers v Harlow Urban District Council (4.8/figure4.3); The Calliope (4.9/figure 4.4). Cases in which a finding of joint fault/contributory negligence could potentially have been made include McKew v Holland Hannen and Cubitts (Scotland) Ltd (4.7); Burrows v March Gas & Coke Co (4.18); The Wagon Mound (No 1) (4.22 and footnote at 4.23).

Government of Ceylon v Chandris (6.21-23/figure 6.4) is a case in which a finding of joint fault (although perhaps not 'contributory negligence') may have been appropriate.

[19] 'Failure to mitigate' loss arising from the breach is a distinct duty situation (2.31/4.13).

The claimant may also be under a separate duty owed to the alleged wrongdoer. A pedestrian and the driver of a vehicle, for example, each owes to the other a duty of care (to avoid collision): Nance v British Columbia Electric Railway Co Ltd [1951] AC 601; [1951] 2 All ER 448, PC. In a road accident case involving a pedestrian and a driver, the driver would (in a joint fault situation) raise contributory negligence in his 'defence' to the 'claim' for damages for personal injury. If the driver had

liability can be apportioned under the Law Reform (Contributory Negligence) Act 1945. S.1(1) of the Act provides that:

> "Where any person suffers damage as the result partly of his own fault and partly of the fault of any other person or persons, a claim in respect of that damage shall not be defeated by reason of the fault of the person suffering the damage, but the damages recoverable in respect thereof shall be reduced to such extent as the Court thinks just and equitable having regard to the claimant's share in the responsibility for the damage."

3.10 S.4 of the Act provides that:

> "Fault means negligence, breach of statutory duty or other act or omission which gives rise to a liability in tort or would, apart from this Act, give rise to the defence of contributory negligence:"

3.11 Contributory negligence in contract. The effect of s.4 of the act is that a (statutory) defence of contributory negligence can only be raised in contract if the wrongdoer is under a 'concurrent duty' (1.12) in tort/delict, that is "where the defendant's liability in contract is the same as his liability in the tort of negligence independently of the existence of any

---

suffered loss/damage he would recover this by way of a 'counterclaim' against the claimant. The claimant would raise a defence of contributory negligence in his 'defence to counterclaim.'

contract."[20] In addition, therefore, to proving that the situation is one of joint fault (2.21-end) and that apportionment of liability is appropriate, it must also be established that the particular type of joint fault is within the ambit of the 1945 Act.[21]

---

[20] Forsikringsaktieselskapet Vesta v Butcher [1988] 3 WLR 565; [1988] 2 All ER 488 at 508f-g, CA. See also Barclays Bank plc v Fairclough Building Ltd and Others (1994) 68 BLR 1, CA at 21 G/C; [1995] 1 All ER 289, CA, considered at 2.32.

Note that the Civil Liability Contribution Act 1979 (3.8) applies "whatever the legal basis of ... liability..": s6(1).

[21] A problem could potentially arise in the case of a 'non-negligent' breach of an express term of the contract. Alternatively the problem could arise if apportionment of liability was appropriate in a situation in which it was not possible to eliminate a concurrent cause by application of the 'first in time' rule (2.9).

Chapter 4

LIABILITY FOR CONSEQUENTIAL ACTS AND EVENTS[1]

a. Introduction

4.1 **The issue.** An act or event is a consequence of a breach if it would not have been a factor at all 'but for' the breach.[2] Whether the original wrongdoer should be liable for such consequences is the issue which is being considered here.[3] The issues of law are very closely related, if not identical, to those raised on a question of 'foreseeability' of type/kind of damage (chapter 5).

4.2 **Chain of events/causation/liability.** If a consequential act or event is found to be attributable to the breach the 'chain of causation' is not broken and the wrongdoer will be liable for the cumulative loss (figure 4.1). In the case of consequential 'acts'/failure to act (4.4) a finding of 'joint fault' may be appropriate if there was negligence on the part of the party performing the consequential act.[4]

---

[1] Often referred to as 'intervening acts and events.'

[2] Illustrated, for example, by Monarch Steamship Co Limited v Karlshamns Oljefabriker (A/B) (4.19).

[3] The issue is in other words whether the 'chain of causation' has been broken.

[4] Examples include Sayers v Harlow Urban District Council (4.8/figure 4.3); The Calliope (4.9/figure 4.4). In The Wagon Mound (No1) there was potential joint liability (contributory negligence) on the part of the owners of the wharf (4.22-23). Burrows v March Gas & Coke Co (4.18) is a case

43

Fig 4.1: Consequential act or event is attributable to the breach

(Wrongdoer is liable for the cumulative damage
if the 'chain of causation' has not been broken).

4.3 **Breaking the chain/new cause.** If, on the other hand, the subsequent factor is not attributable to the breach then the chain of causation is said to have been broken and the wrongdoer will only be liable for any initial damage caused by the breach and not in respect of any further damage attributable to the consequential act or event (figure 4.2). In such circumstances the consequential act or event may be referred to as a 'new and independent cause'[5] of damage. The effect could be as in figure 2.3, that is separate causes of distinct damage.

---

involving a third party in which a finding of joint fault could potentially have been made.

Note that an element of 'negligence' may be excusable (4.4).

[5] Sometimes referred to as a 'novus actus interveniens.'

Fig 4.2: Consequential act or event is not attributable to the breach

(The 'chain of causation' is said to have been broken and the wrongdoer is relieved of liability for any <u>further</u> damage)

b. Liability for Consequential Acts

4.4   Test. In the case of a consequential act[6]/failure to act[7] the wrongdoer will be liable if the injured party acted reasonably (by what he did or by what he failed to do) in the circumstances in which he was placed as a result of the

---

[6] These include, for example, acceleration measures taken by a contractor in an attempt to mitigate delay caused by employer's default or actions by the master of a ship in an attempt to save her following a collision at sea. Acts of third parties generally fall into the category of consequential 'events' (chapter 4 part d).

[7] The test is the same where the allegation is one of 'failure to act.' A failure to act may consist of a breach of an implied common law/contractual duty such as in the case of Lambert and another v Lewis and others [1982] AC 225, [1981] 2 WLR 713; [1981] 1 All ER 1185, HL. Alternatively it may consist of a breach of the 'duty to mitigate' loss, a special type of duty situation, considered in part c of this chapter. The distinction between an ordinary implied duty and the duty to mitigate is considered at 4.13.

breach.[8] The burden of proof is on the wrongdoer to show that the claimant's actions were unreasonable in the circumstances.[9]

4.5   The Metagama[10] concerned an action arising out of a collision between 2 vessels on the river Clyde. It was alleged that the master of the claimant's vessel had been negligent in that he had failed to keep the engines running after 'beaching.' This failure had resulted in total loss when the ship slipped into the river Clyde.[11] On the facts, the master of the ship was not negligent and there was no break in the chain of causation (initiated by the collision)/no new and independent cause. The relevant principle of law was stated in the following terms by Viscount Haldane (at p254):

"...what those in charge of the injured ship do to save

---

[8] In order to reconcile this with the principles applicable on a question of 'foreseeability,' it could be said that only reasonable acts of the claimant will be held to be within the reasonable contemplation of/reasonably foreseeable by the wrongdoer.

[9] Roper v Johnson (1873) LR 8 CP 167; The onus was described as being a 'heavy' one by Lord Shaw in The Metagama (4.5) at p259. See also Lord Blanesburgh at p265.
   Note, however that in Selvanayagam v University of the West Indies [1983] 1 All ER 824, PC at 827 it was held that the claimant must prove that in all the circumstances his failure to take the steps in question was reasonable.

[10] (1927) 29 Ll LR 253 (HL), also referred to as Canadian Pacific Ry Co v Kelvin Shipping Co Ld. (1927) 138 L.T. 369.

[11] This is effectively an allegation of failure to mitigate: per Lord Blanesburgh (at p264), Viscount Haldane (at p254) and Viscount Dunedin at p256.

it may be mistaken, but if they do whatever they do reasonably, although unsuccessfully, their mistaken judgment may be a natural consequence for which the offending ship is responsible, just as much as any physical occurrence."[12]

4.6 In McKew v Holland Hannen and Cubitts (Scotland) Ltd[13] the claimant suffered injury to his leg at work as a result of his employer's negligence. Some time thereafter his leg gave way when he was about to descend a staircase. In an attempt to save himself (which would not have been an unreasonable act on his part) he jumped onto the lower landing and sustained a further severe injury to his ankle. The chain of causation was said to have been broken before his leg had given way and before he was forced to jump, however, since it was unreasonable for the him, when his leg had given way on other occasions since the accident, to attempt to descend a steep staircase which had no handrail without seeking adult assistance. The employer was not therefore liable for the further injury.[14]

4.7 **Chain not broken but finding of joint fault.** As an alternative to a finding that either one party or the other should be wholly responsible for the damage in question, a finding of joint fault could be considered. This may be appropriate if the claimant's actions in consequence of the

---

[12] This was referred to as an important statement of principle by Lord Wright in The Oropesa [1943] P. 32 at p40.

[13] 1969 SC 14; [1969] 3 All ER 1621, HL

[14] This is a case in which a finding of joint fault (involving 'contributory negligence') could potentially have been made (4.7).

breach were negligent (in the circumstances)[15] but not so negligent as to lead to a conclusion that the chain of causation had been broken.

4.8   The case of Sayers v Harlow Urban District Council[16] (figure 4.3) concerned an action for breach of duty (negligence) pursuant to an implied contract and/or tort/delict. The claimant, having paid to use the amenity, found herself locked inside a public toilet as there was no handle on the inside of the door. This was a 'latent' breach by the council(figures 2.8 and 2.9). The claimant attempted to climb out by standing on the toilet and then placing one foot on the toilet roll and fixture. On discovering that she would be unable to climb out she attempted to descend at which point the toilet roll rotated causing her to fall and injure herself. To attempt to climb out was reasonable in the circumstances and that was therefore a consequence in respect of which the council were liable (the chain of causation had not been broken). Damages were reduced by 25%, however, since the claimant was found to have been careless in the process of returning to the ground by allowing her balance to depend on the toilet roll.

---

[15] It may be that a finding of contributory negligence would be less likely than it would be in the case of 'non-consequential' acts. 'Allowance' is made for the fact that the claimant is in a position of difficulty as a result of the breach.

[16] [1958] 1 WLR 623; [1958] 2 All ER 342, CA

Fig 4.3: Sayers v Harlow UDC

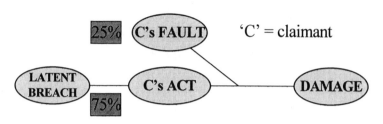

4.9   In The Calliope[17] (figure 4.4) the initial collision was caused by the fault of both ships (45% plaintiff and 55% defendant). This was followed some time later by further damage due to the defendant's negligent, 'consequential' manoeuvre on the river.

Fig 4.4: The Calliope

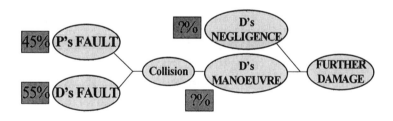

As to whether a further 'sub-apportionment' of liability was appropriate, Brandon J stated that:[18]

---

[17] Carlsholm (Owners) v Calliope (Owners), The Calliope [1970] P 172; [1970] 2 WLR 991; [1970] 1 All ER 624.

[18] [1970] P 172 at 184F.

"...it is open to the court, as a matter of law, in a case like the present, to find that the alleged consequential damage was caused partly by the original casualty, and partly by the claimant's own intervening negligence, and to make a further sub-apportionment of liability accordingly."

He also said that "..it is only right to add that I express it with some diffidence" and in any event that:

"...cases where it would be right to find that such damage was caused both by such intervening negligence and by the original negligence which resulted in the casualty may well be comparatively rare. They will certainly be much less frequent than cases of joint fault based on successive acts of negligence both of which precede the original casualty."[19]

c. Duty to mitigate

4.10 Principle. One of the 'consequences' of a breach of duty is the imposition of a legal duty upon the claimant to take reasonable steps to avoid/mitigate his loss. In the British Westinghouse Electric case[20] Viscount Haldane LC stated that:

"The fundamental basis is thus compensation for

---

[19] A similar situation arose in the case of Government of Ceylon v Chandris (6.21-23).

[20] British Westinghouse Electric and Manufacturing Co Ltd v Underground Electric Railways Co of London Ltd [1912] AC 673; [1911–13] All ER Rep 63

pecuniary loss naturally flowing from the breach [(1.2)]; but this first principle is qualified by a second, which imposes on a plaintiff the duty of taking all reasonable steps to mitigate the loss consequent on the breach, and debars him from claiming any part of the damage which is due to[21] his neglect to take such steps. In the words of James L.J. in *Dunkirk Colliery Co. v. Lever* ((1878) 9 Ch D 20 at 25), "The person who has broken the contract is not to be exposed to additional cost by reason of the plaintiffs not doing what they ought to have done as reasonable men, and the plaintiffs not being under any obligation to do anything otherwise than in the ordinary course of business." As James L.J. indicates, this second principle does not impose on the plaintiff an obligation to take any step which a reasonable and prudent man would not ordinarily take in the course of his business. But when in the course of his business he has taken action arising out of the transaction, which action has diminished his loss, the effect in actual diminution of the loss he has suffered may be taken into account even though there was no duty on him to act."[22]

4.11 Burden of proof. The party who asserts that the whole or part of the damage ought to have been avoided bears the burden of proof on that issue (4.4).

4.12 Test to be applied. The test is considered at 4.4.

---

[21] 'Due to' = 'caused by.'

[22] [1912] AC 673 at 688–689, [1911–13] All ER Rep 63 at 69.

4.13 'Duty to mitigate' and other implied terms/duties distinguished. The legal basis for the imposition of a 'duty to mitigate,' whether arising in contract or in tort/delict, is 'foreseeability of loss/injury.' In this regard the duty is the same as any other implied 'term'/duty (contract or tort/delict) of this nature.

In the contractual context there would (generally)[23] be no implied term/duty (that is, other than the 'duty to mitigate') on the part of the claimant to avoid incurring loss as a result of another's breach (2.29-31).

4.14 Where, however, such a implied term/duty does co-exist with the duty to mitigate then, as stated above, the legal basis is the same in each case. This is despite the fact that the 'defences' have different 'labels' attached to them and the fact that the relevant duties arise at different times. A 'duty to mitigate' loss (associated with the defence of 'failure to mitigate') generally only arises *after* the relevant breach has occurred. The duty arises, however, at the point when loss injury becomes 'reasonably foreseeable' as a result of a breach of duty and it could therefore arise before the relevant breach. In Barclays Bank plc v Fairclough Building Ltd and Others Beldam LJ stated that:

> "To be regarded as negligent in law, conduct must involve a failure to guard against a risk which is reasonably foreseeable. If the conduct relied on consists of an omission to guard against the failure of another person to carry out his legal obligations, it must be established that experience shows such failure to be

---

[23] This does not generally apply in the case of the claimant's duty to avoid personal injury to himself (2.29).

likely.[24] Further, to be negligent the conduct must be unreasonable in all the circumstances."[25]

4.15 A duty to avoid loss arising from an implied term/duty (associated with the defence of 'contributory negligence') exists *before* the breach occurs. The relevant negligence may however arise after the breach, that is in the case of a latent or continuing breach.[26]

4.16 **Joint fault arising out of a 'failure to mitigate.'** 'Failure to mitigate' is generally regarded as an 'all or nothing' defence. 'Joint fault' and 'apportionment of liability' are not, therefore, generally considered.[27] 'Apportionment of liability' could potentially be appropriate if the claimant's action/inaction in consequence of the breach involved a breach of duty/fault/negligence which was insufficient to 'break the chain' and make him fully liable.

d. Liability for Consequential Events.

4.17 **Nature of consequential events.** An occurrence is a 'consequential' event if it would not have been a factor at all

---

[24] Illustrated by the case of Schering Agrochemicals Ltd v Resibel NVSA [1992] CA Transcript 1298 (in which there had been an earlier breach of contract), considered in County Ltd and another v Girozentrale Securities [1996] 3 All ER 801, CA.

[25] [1995] 1 All ER 279, CA at 299h-j.

[26] Illustrated by Sayers v Harlow UDC (figure 4.3).

[27] If the defence is successful the claimant's action/inaction is regarded as 'the' cause of damage (figure 4.2). This is the same, in effect, as a finding of 100% contributory negligence.

'but for' the breach. This category is concerned with any occurrence which is not in the category of a consequential 'act' of the claimant (4.4).

4.18 Examples of consequential events. Examples include 'knock-on effects' of the breach, acts of god,[28] outbreak of war, strikes by workmen,[29] fire, explosion and acts of independent third parties.[30]

In a construction contract it would not be uncommon for a 'neutral event,'[31] such as bad weather[32] or a strike by

---

[28] Flood, lightning, typhoon, earthquake and the like.

[29] In HMS London [1914] P. 72, a wrongdoer who had caused a collision at sea was held to be liable further loss arising due to a strike by dockworkers occurring during the repair of the damaged ship.

[30] Illustrated by Home Office v Dorset Yacht Co Ltd [1970] AC 1004; [1970] 2 WLR 1140; [1970] 2 All ER 294, HL. In Burrows v March Gas & Coke Co (1870) LR 5 Exch. 67, a gas company, in breach of their contract, supplied a defective pipe. There was an escape of gas and a third party went negligently to investigate with a lighted candle (the consequential act/event). The gas company was held liable in full for the damage. A finding of joint fault could, however, have been made due to the negligence on the part of the party investigating the escape of gas.

[31] Neutral events are events which might foreseeably affect progress but which are generally outwith the control of either party. Accordingly a provision for extension of time may be made in the contract but any loss attributable to the event will generally not be recoverable from the other party.

[32] See Colman J in Balfour Beatty Building Ltd v Chestermount Properties Ltd (2.13) at 34-35, concerning the situation where the contractor is in culpable delay and the works are further delayed, eg by a storm and flooding which would, but for the non-completion, have been avoided altogether. At p35 he said: "In such a case it is hard to see that it would be fair and reasonable to postpone the completion date to extend the

workmen[33] to further affect progress during a period of culpable delay.[34]

4.19 Test. The test is whether the wrongdoer ought[35] to have contemplated/foreseen the occurrence of the event[36] and, if so, he will be liable for any damage/further damage caused thereby.

In Monarch Steamship Co Limited v Karlshamns Oljefabriker (A/B),[37] the leading case in contract, the owner's breach in providing an unseaworthy vessel necessitated diversion for repair. 'But for' this delay to the voyage the vessel would have reached her Swedish destination before outbreak of the second world war. As a result of the outbreak of war she was ordered by the British Admiralty to proceed to Glasgow. The owner was held liable for the further delay

---

contractor's time."

[33] See judgment of HHJ Fox-Andrews in Fairweather (H) & Co Ltd v London Borough of Wandsworth (2.16) at 118-119 - example of direct loss and expense being recoverable by the contractor where strikes (normally a neutral event) cause further delay during a period of culpable delay by the employer.

[34] 'Culpable delay' is a period of delay which is the fault of one of the parties and in respect of which that party is liable to pay damages.

[35] The test is an 'objective' one, that is 'whether a reasonable man in the position of the wrongdoer' would have contemplated/foreseen the occurrence of the event (5.2-5.4).

[36] Monarch Steamship Co Limited v Karlshamns Oljefabriker (A/B) [1949] AC 196, HL. Note that, for the reasons stated at 5.9 no reference has been made to 'risk'/'likelihood'/'probability of occurrence.

[37] [1949] AC 196; [1949] 1 All ER, 1, HL.

caused by the war/diversion to Glasgow (the consequential event) and for the costs of transhipment to Sweden. At p216, Lord Porter said that:

> "..the diversion to Glasgow, brought about through the delay in carrying out the contract of carriage in the present case, is attributable to the default of the owners of the ship, because in the conditions existing in April, 1939, they ought to have foreseen[38] that war might shortly break out and that any prolongation of the voyage might cause the loss of or diversion of the ship."

4.20 'Foreseeability' is a question of fact. This point is considered at 5.3.

4.21 Imputed knowledge/knowledge of technical matters. Whether the wrongdoer should be taken to have contemplated/foreseen the occurrence of the event depends on knowledge of matters, which may include matters of a 'technical' nature, which he had or ought to have had (also considered at 5.5).

4.22 This point is well illustrated by two contrasting decisions of

---

[38] There is no distinction between 'foreseen' and 'contemplated' in this context (5.2). The remaining Law Lords based their decisions on what the owner ought to have 'contemplated.' At p233-4 Lord Uthwatt stated that "a reasonable shipowner contemplating a voyage ..." At p234 Lord Du Parc stated that: "...It is enough if they may reasonably be assumed to have contemplated a war, ..." Lord Morton stated, at p235: "In my view, the damage which was in fact suffered by the respondents was within the reasonable contemplation of the parties,..." At p222 Lord Wright stated that "risks consequent on the prolongation of the voyage must have been in contemplation both by the shipowners and the shippers."

the Privy Council arising out of the same set of circumstances. The circumstances were that, as a result of the negligence of engineers on board the vessel The Wagon Mound, a large quantity of furnace oil was spilt onto the surface of the waters in Sydney Harbour. The oil drifted into a wharf where the plaintiffs (in the first action) were working and caught fire as a consequence of an act of manager of the plaintiffs in resuming oxy-acetylene welding and cutting while the wharf was surrounded by oil.[39] The fire caused extensive damage to the wharf and to vessels moored therein. The first action, The Wagon Mound (No 1),[40] was brought by the owners of the wharf in the torts of negligence and nuisance.[41] One of the findings of fact was that the wrongdoers did not know and could not reasonably have been expected to know that the furnace oil was capable of being set alight when spread on water as they **could not have had** the necessary technical knowledge at the material time. It was held that, although pollution was a foreseeable consequence of the spillage, an outbreak of fire was not.

4.23 In the second action, The Wagon Mound (No 2),[42] however,

---

[39] The 'act' of the manager was not a 'consequence of' the spillage so the issue is one concerning a consequential 'event' (4.17). The consequential 'event' was the fire, caused by the welding/decision to recommence same.

[40] Overseas Tankship (UK) Ltd v Morts Dock & Engineering Co Ltd, The Wagon Mound (No1) [1961] AC 388; [1961] 2 WLR 126; [1961] 1 Lloyd's Rep 1; [1961] 1 All ER 404, PC; [1961] ALR 569.

[41] The decision of the Privy Council was concerned with the claim in negligence only.

[42] Overseas Tankship (UK) Ltd v The Miller Steamship Co Pty Ltd and Another, The Wagon Mound (No 2) [1967] 1 AC 617; [1966] 3 WLR 498; [1966] 1 Lloyd's Rep 657; [1966] 2 All ER 709, PC. The second

the trial judge held that the engineers knew or ought to have known that it would be possible, although very difficult to set the furnace oil alight and that it would rarely happen/happen only in exceptional circumstances.[43] With the trial judge's findings in mind Lord Reid said that:

"It follows that in their lordships view the only question is whether a reasonable man having the knowledge and experience to be expected of the chief engineer of the Wagon Mound would have known that there was a real risk of the oil on the water catching fire in some way"[44]

The answer to the question was 'yes' and the outbreak of fire was, therefore, attributable to the owners of the Wagon Mound.

---

action was commenced by the owners of vessels moored in the wharf, again in negligence and nuisance. It was held that the same test of reasonable foreseeability, as applies to actions in negligence, applies to actions in nuisance: per Lord Reid at [1966] 2 All ER 709 at 717.

[43] The findings of fact were materially different as a result of differences in the evidence led by the plaintiffs in the first action. Lord Porter explained this as follows ([1966] 2 All ER 709, at 717 PC):
"So if the plaintiffs in the former case had set out to prove that it was foreseeable by the engineers of the Wagon Mound that this oil could be set alight, they might have had difficulty in parrying the reply that then this must also have been foreseeable by their manager. Then there would have been contributory negligence and at that time contributory negligence was a complete defence in New South Wales."

[44] [1966] 2 All ER 709 at 718-719. The words 'real risk' are a reference to 'remoteness' of damage (5.9). The issue could be expressed as being 'whether the engineer ought to have foreseen the outbreak of fire."

4.24 Knowledge of 'specialist' technical matters relevant to the claimant's business. This point is considered at 5.5.

4.25 Relevance of 'risk of occurrence'/'remoteness' to foreseeability. This is considered at 5.9.

Chapter 5

FORESEEABILITY OF TYPE/KIND OF LOSS

5.1 **Introduction.** 'Foreseeability' is the criteria for determining whether a 'type/kind' of loss is recoverable from the wrongdoer.[1] 'Unforeseeable' types/kinds of loss are not recoverable.

'Exceptions' to foreseeability principles, such as whether there is a duty of care in respect of 'economic loss' and other 'policy considerations,' are out with the scope of this book.[2]

5.2 **Test of foreseeability.** The test/underlying principle is the same as in the case of consequential acts and events (chapter 4). The question is whether the type/kind of loss consequent upon the breach ought to have been[3] in the contemplation

---

[1] The issue is commonly referred to as one of 'remoteness of damage' (5.9).

[2] In the case of a claim for 'interest,' as a result of late payment in contract, ambiguity can arise due to the fact that a claim for 'interest' can take a variety of forms. If the claim is for loss actually incurred (such as bank interest/finance charges) then foreseeability principles apply. The decision in the London, Chatham and Dover Rly Co v South Eastern Rly Co [1893] AC 429, HL does not apply to such a claim since none of the 4 types of interest considered in that case involved incurrence of actual loss. The principles considered herein (at 1.2 and in relation to foreseeability) were not therefore relevant/considered in that case.

[3] The test is an objective one: ".... it suffices that if he had considered the question he would as a reasonable man have concluded that the loss in question was liable to result." Per Lord Morris of Borth y Gest in The Heron II [1967] 3 All ER at 700-701 and per Lord Reid at [1967] 3 All ER at 691, considered below.

of/foreseen by[4] the party in breach at the date of the contract/tort.[5,6]

If the type/kind of damage/occurrence is one which the wrongdoer ought to have foreseen then he will, subject to the duty to mitigate loss (chapter 4 part c), be liable for the whole loss attributable to the breach regardless of the extent thereof.[7]

---

[4] There is no distinction between 'contemplated,' which is commonly used in the contractual context, and 'foreseen,' which is generally used in the context of tort/delict. Although this position may have been modified by the terms of the particular contract, The Heron II (5.6) refers, the test is otherwise the same in contract and in tort/delict: Lords Denning and Scarman in Parsons (H) (Livestock) Ltd v Uttley Ingham & Co Ltd [1978] 1 All ER 525, [1978] QB 791, [1977] 3 WLR 990, CA. In Banque Bruxelles Lambert SA v Eagle Star Insurance Co Ltd and others and other appeals [1995] 2 All ER 769, CA at 841 Sir Thomas Bingham MR said that:

"Somewhat different language has been used to define the test in contract and tort, but the essence of the test is the same in each case. The test is whether, at the date of the contract or tort, damage of the kind for which the plaintiff claims compensation was a reasonably foreseeable consequence of the breach of contract or tortious conduct of which the plaintiff complains."

[5] In the leading case in tort/delict, The Wagon Mound (No.1) [1961] AC 388, 426; [1961] 1 All ER 404, 415 (4.22), Viscount Simonds said that:

"The essential factor in determining liability is whether the damage is of such a kind as the reasonable man should have foreseen."

[6] Foreseeability is to be determined at the time of the occurrence of the wrong (tort/delict) or at the date of the agreement (contract). The wrongdoer will not therefore be liable if, for example, essential technical or other information relevant to his knowledge was not available to him at that time.

[7] Parsons (H) (Livestock) Ltd v Uttley Ingham & Co Ltd [1978] QB 791; [1978] 3 WLR 990; [1978] 1 All ER 525 CA.

5.3 **Foreseeability is a question of fact.** Whether the wrongdoer ought to be taken to have foreseen the type/kind of loss/occurrence of the event depends on his knowledge (express or implied). The knowledge which the wrongdoer possesses/is deemed to possess depends on all the circumstances of the case. Foreseeability is therefore an issue of fact/there can be no 'test' as to whether a particular kind of loss/occurrence is foreseeable (5.10).

5.4 **Matters relevant to knowledge/foreseeability.** Relevant matters include the type of contract (or relationship where the action is in tort/delict), the nature of the wrongdoer's and/or of the claimant's business. If 'special knowledge' is required to make a type of loss/consequence foreseeable, such as in the case of Hadley v Baxendale (5.7), it will be necessary to consider whether there was any express/implied communication of information relevant thereto.

As the test of foreseeability is an objective one it is necessary to consider what a reasonable man[8] in the position of the wrongdoer, would have known in considering what knowledge should be implied. Expert evidence may be relevant in relation to the knowledge which a particular 'reasonable man' ought to have had and/or in relation to technical matters such as would have been considered in the Wagon Mound cases (4.22-23).

5.5 **Contracts between businessmen.** As to when knowledge will be imputed in a contract between businessmen, Lord Wright said that:

"... the question in a case like the present must always

---

[8] For example, a reasonable engineer (Wagon Mound), carrier of goods (Hadley v Baxendale).

be what reasonable business men must be taken to have contemplated as the natural or probable result if the contract was broken. As reasonable business men each must be taken to understand the **ordinary practices and exigencies** of the other's trade or business. That need not generally be the subject of special discussion or communication."[9]

5.6   In the Heron II[10] a vessel was chartered for the carriage by sea of 3000 tons of sugar. As a result of the owner's breach of contract there was a 9 day delay in arriving at Basrah, the port of destination. Had the vessel arrived on time the charterers would have obtained £32 10s per ton for the sugar rather than £31 2s 9d as they were in fact able to. The owners were aware that there was a market for sugar in Basrah but were unaware that there was an intention to sell. It was held that the owner ought reasonably to have foreseen the type/kind of loss, that is 'loss of profits due to a fall in market value.'

5.7   Communication of 'special/out of the ordinary'[11]

---

[9] Monarch Steamship Co Ltd v Karlshamns Oljefabriker (A/B) [1949] AC 196, 224; [1949] 1 All ER 1, 14, HL (4.19).

[10] Koufos v Czarnikow Ltd (The Heron II) [1969] 1 AC 350; [1967] 3 All ER 686, HL

[11] 'Special/out of the ordinary' circumstances are those which would be generally unforeseeable by the parties to the type of contract in question. Such matters must communicated to the other party. A distinction is therefore created between 'ordinary' facts/circumstances (5.5) and 'special' facts/circumstances. There is no distinction, however, between 'different types of damages' (commonly referred to as 'general' and 'special' damages). In the Monarch Steamship case (4.19) Lord Wright said that:

"The ruling of Alderson B [in Hadley v Baxendale] has consistently

circumstances. In Hadley v Baxendale[12] the owners of a flour mill entered into a contract with a carrier of goods for the delivery of a broken crank shaft to engineers who had the task of making a new one. Although the mill could not operate without the shaft, this fact was not communicated to the carrier. There was a 5 day delay in delivery caused by a breach by the courier and this meant an additional 5 days loss of profits amounting to £300. As to whether the delay ought reasonably to have been in the contemplation of the courier at the date of the contract, Alderson B said that:

"... we find that the only circumstances here communicated by the plaintiffs to the defendants at the time the contract was made were that the article to be carried was the broken shaft of a mill and that the plaintiffs were the millers of that mill. But how do these circumstances show reasonably that the profits of the mill must be stopped by an unreasonable delay in the delivery of the broken shaft by the carrier to the third person? Suppose the plaintiffs had another shaft in their possession put up or putting up at the time, and that they only wished to send back the broken shaft to the engineer who made it; it is clear that this would be quite consistent with the above circumstances, and yet

---

been followed. The only difficulty, as Lord Sankey observes, has been in applying it. The distinction there drawn is between damages arising naturally (which means in the normal course of things) and cases where there were special and extraordinary circumstances beyond the reasonable prevision of the parties. In the latter event it is laid down that the special facts must be communicated by and between the parties." [1949] 1 All ER at 12.

[12] (1854), 9 Exch 341; [1843–60] All ER Rep 461; 23 LJEx 179, 23 LTOS 69, 156 ER 145.

the unreasonable delay in the delivery would have no effect upon the intermediate profits of the mill. Or, again, suppose that at the time of the delivery to the carrier the machinery of the mill had been in other respects defective, then, also the same results would follow."[13]

In conclusion Alderson B stated that:

"It follows, therefore, that the loss of profits here cannot reasonably be considered such a consequence of the breach of contract as could have been fairly and reasonably contemplated by both the parties when they made this contract."[14]

5.8   In Victoria Laundry (Windsor) Ltd v Newman Industries Ltd[15] there was a delay in the supply of a boiler to the laundry and as a consequence the laundry company lost the opportunity to enter into some highly lucrative dyeing contracts which they would otherwise have been in a position to do. The 'exceptional profits' were not recoverable as the prospect of the dyeing contracts had not been communicated to the supplier at the date of the supply contract. Ordinary business

---

[13] (1854), 9 Exch 341 at 355; [1843–60] All ER Rep 461 at 465-466.

As foreseeability is a question of fact different judges are likely to have different reasoning and would be likely to give different weight to different types of evidence. It could alternatively have been reasoned that a 'reasonable courier' may not have been aware of the significance of a crank shaft to the operation of a mill whereas an engineer or supplier would perhaps have been.

[14] (1854), 9 Exch 341 at 356; [1843–60] All ER Rep 461 at 466.

[15] [1949] 2 KB 528; [1949] 1 All ER 997, CA.

profits were however recoverable.[16,17]

5.9 Relevance of 'probability/risk' of occurrence ('remoteness' of damage). If the 'probability/risk/likelihood' of something occurring is 'remote' then it has only a 'slight' or 'faint' chance of occurring. When a type/kind of loss is said to be 'too remote to be recoverable' it means that the 'probability/risk' of the loss being incurred was so slight that the wrongdoer ought not to be taken to have contemplated/foreseen it.

Whether the wrongdoer ought to have foreseen the type/kind of loss/occurrence of the event does not, however, depend upon the **degree of 'probability/risk'** of its occurrence.[18] The issue is whether the wrongdoer ought to

---

[16] In the Monarch Steamship case, Lord Wright said that:
"Alderson B then points out that, if the special circumstances of the particular case were wholly unknown to the other party, he could at most be only supposed to contemplate the amount of injury which would arise generally and in the great number of cases not affected by any special circumstances." [1949] 1 All ER at 12.

[17] If the performance of a construction contract is delayed by employer's breach and the contractor makes a claim for 'lost opportunity' to earn profit on other contracts then he would be entitled to recover ordinary business profits which similar companies would earn in similar transactions. The tender allowance or previous years' accounting information may be admissible as evidence of such ordinary profits. In order to recover an amount in excess of 'ordinary' profits special facts/information would have to be communicated at the date of the contract.

[18] The 'degree of risk/chance' of something occurring and/or the 'assessment' thereof may be relevant to the issue as to whether a 'duty of care' should be imposed: Bolton v Stone [1951] AC 850; [1951] 1 All ER 1078, HL (considered in The Wagon Mound (No2)). A 'breach of duty' is, however, to be assumed in considering 'foreseeability of the type/kind

have been aware of it/foreseen it.[19]

In Hadley v Baxendale there was no issue as to a 'degree of risk' of a delay in operating the mill occurring.[20] Even if

---

of damage.'

In The Heron II Lord Morris said that: "I cannot think that he [the wrongdoer] should escape liability by saying that he would only be aware of a possibility of loss but not of a probability or certainty of it:" [1967] 3 All ER at 699, HL. Otherwise it could be inferred that a wrongdoer would be entitled to make an assessment of risk, a matter which received the disapproval of Lords Porter and Normand in Bolton v Stone.

[19] If the matter in question could not possibly have been foreseen then the wrongdoer will not be liable in respect of it. In The Wagon Mound (No2) (4.23) Lord Reid said that:

"It has now been established by the Wagon Mound (No 1) and by Hughes v Lord Advocate that in such cases damages can only be recovered if the injury complained of not only was caused by the alleged negligence but also was an injury of a class or character **foreseeable as a possible result of it**."

[20] This case is generally regarded as the source of the 'remoteness' theory. The inference that degree of risk was material may be derived from the reasoning of Alderson B (leading up to the conclusion that the delay was not foreseeable) at (1854), 9 Exch at p 356; [1843–60] All ER Rep at p 466:

"But it is obvious that, in the great multitude of cases of millers sending off broken shafts to third persons by a carrier under ordinary circumstances, such consequences **would not, in all probability, have occurred**."

Alderson B then concluded that the consequence could not therefore have been in the contemplation of the parties (5.7). It can be concluded therefore that in this context a 'probable' occurrence = a 'foreseeable' one and that the foregoing sentence could therefore be taken to mean that 'in this type of contract, such consequences would not, generally, be foreseeable/in the contemplation of the parties.' The words 'would not, in all probability, have occurred' could therefore be regarded as a reference to the standard of proof (the balance of probabilities) on the issue of foreseeability rather than as a reference to probability/risk (in the degree of risk had been a factor, it could not have been a material/decisive one because the carrier would have been liable for the delay if he had known/ought to have known that the replacement shaft was necessary to operate the mill.[21]

5.10 To attempt to lay down an all embracing rule as to foreseeability is like trying to define the point at which the balance of probabilities lies. The issue is one of fact and the reasoning of judges on the issue of foreseeability will inevitably be different. In the Monarch Steamship case, Lord Wright approved of Lord Haldane's view of the problem. His Lordship said that:

> "The question whether damage is remote or "natural" and direct[22] can in general only be decided on a review of the circumstances of each special case. Remoteness of damage[23] is, in truth, a question of fact, as Lord Haldane LC describes it in the British Westinghouse case. He said ([1912] AC 688) with reference to questions as to damages:

---

remoteness sense) that something might occur.

[21] If the mill was being constructed, however, the supplier of an essential part (or the sub-contractor carrying out the installation of the part) may have been liable for the delay because delay is (generally) a foreseeable consequence of late performance of a construction contract. It may be that foreseeability can be inferred from the nature of the contract alone. In construction contracts however the supplier/sub-contractor may in addition have been given tender drawings, main contract information, delivery dates etc.

[22] These words are used to distinguish unforeseeable and foreseeable losses/events.

[23] 'Remoteness of damage' in this context means 'foreseeability.'

"In some of the cases there are expressions as to the principles governing the measure of general damages which at first sight seem difficult to harmonise. The apparent discrepancies are, however, mainly due to the varying nature of the particular questions submitted for decision. The quantum of damage is a question of fact, and the only guidance the law can give is to lay down general principles which afford at times but scanty assistance in dealing with particular cases. The judges who give guidance to juries in these cases have necessarily to look at their special character, and to mould, for the purposes of different kinds of claim, the expression of the general principles which apply to them, and this is apt to give rise to an appearance of ambiguity."[24]

---

[24] Monarch Steamship Co Ltd v Karlshamns Oljefabriker (A/B) [1949] AC 196 at 223; [1949] 1 All ER 1 at 13, HL. See also Lord du Parc [1949] AC at p 232; [1949] 1 All ER at p 19 and Lord Morris of Borth-y-Gest in The Heron II [1967] 3 All ER at 699.

Chapter 6

ASSESSMENT OF DAMAGES

a. Generally

6.1 **Introduction.** This chapter is concerned with the rules which govern the assessment[1] of the 'amount/quantum' of damages, that is the 'extent of' the wrongdoer's liability.

6.2 **Amount/quantum is a question of fact.** As with 'foreseeability' (5.3) and 'causation' (2.2), the amount/quantum of damages to which the claimant is entitled is a question of fact.[2]

6.3 **Underlying principle.** In all cases, damages should be assessed on the basis of the underlying principle as stated at 1.2 (A=C-B). The amount of the claimant's entitlement (A) is sometimes referred to as the 'measure of damages.'

6.4 **Burden and standard of proof.** A claimant seeking to recover damages must adduce evidence from which the tribunal of fact (the judge/arbitrator in a civil case) can infer that, on the balance of probabilities, some kind of injury/harm has occurred. If it cannot be inferred from the evidence that the claimant has suffered injury/harm of any kind then, unless the situation is one in which a presumption of injury/harm is made (6.9), the claimant will have failed to discharge the

---

[1] 'Assess,' 'quantify' and 'ascertain' have the same meaning in this context.

[2] per Viscount Haldane in the British Westinghouse case and Lord Wright in the Monarch Steamship case (5.10)

burden of proof and should recover no damages.[3]

The claimant is entitled to recover the 'amount' which he has, on the balance of probabilities, suffered as a result of the breach, that is, the amount which can be reasonably inferred/assessed from the evidence adduced.

b. Pleading

6.5   Matters relevant to the claim must be particularised. The claimant should in his pleading/statement of claim, state particulars of any 'specific' loss/injury alleged to have been caused by the breach and of any other facts/matters relied on which are material/relevant to the claim for damages.[4] The purpose of this requirement is to give the wrongdoer fair warning of the extent of the claim being made against him and the opportunity to make an offer in settlement/payment into court if appropriate.[5] Failure to give the required particulars in the pleading may result in evidence being inadmissible at trial.

6.6   Degree of 'particularity' required. The degree of

---

[3] The term 'nominal' damages is considered at 6.9.

[4] The term 'general damage' is a reference to 'presumed damage,' that is loss/damage which does not have to be pleaded/proved such as in the case of a tort/delict actionable 'per se' (6.9). The term 'special damage' refers to any type of damage which is not presumed and would include for example actual financial loss incurred up to the date of trial (referred to as 'patrimonial loss' in Scotland). Rules of Court may prescribe what matters should and should not be pleaded. 'Special damage' is an ambiguous term: Bowen LJ in Ratcliffe v Evans (6.11-12) at 528.

[5] Ratcliffe v Evans (6.11-12) at p528; Perestrello E Companhia Limitada v United Paint Co Ltd [1969] 3 All ER, 479 (CA).

particularity required is that which, if supported by evidence, would be sufficient to discharge the burden of proof (6.4). It is generally up to the claimant, subject to rules of procedure and evidence, what to plead/what evidence to adduce. As to the degree of particularity possible, this is something which, as in the case of certainty/accuracy (6.7), depends on the circumstances of each case.

c. Assessment

6.7 **Degree of certainty/accuracy possible; the uncertain nature of damages.** The degree of certainty/accuracy possible in the assessment of damages depends upon the circumstances of each case including the nature of the harm done.[6] It may also depend upon "existing knowledge, and ...the degree of accuracy involved in the remainder of the exercise which

---

[6] See for example Chaplin v Hicks (6.10) which concerns a claim for 'lost opportunity.' In Thompson and others v Smiths Shiprepairers (North Shields) Ltd (6.24-26), which concerned a claim for damages for personal injury, Mustill J said (at p905) that:
"........The starting point for any inquiry into the measure of damages is the principle that the court should so far as possible endeavour to restore the plaintiff to the position in which he would have found himself but for the defendant's wrongful act [(1.2)]. The impracticability of giving full effect to this principle must be recognised at every stage of the process. Money can never properly compensate a loss which consists of social impairment rather than financial deprivation. Quantification of damages for personal injury involves the use of conventional measures, the adoption of which at once makes nonsense of any attempts at mathematical accuracy. In a field where the subject matter is people, not contracts, bank balances and abstract rights, the recognition that certain results are unacceptable in human terms must rightly lead to alternative solutions which cannot be easily rationalised. Complete logical rigour cannot be attained."

leads to the computation of damages,"[7] the complexity of the situation[8] and the availability of evidence (6.13-14) such as contemporaneous records of events.[9]

6.8   Degree of certainty/accuracy required; the overriding principle. Neither difficulty of proof nor absolute uncertainty/impossibility of assessing damages with mathematical accuracy[10] will act as a bar to recovery of damages if it is established by the evidence that some

---

[7] Mustill J in Thompson and others v Smiths Shiprepairers (North Shields) Ltd (6.24-26) at p906. Even where the claim is for financial loss and all evidence is available, 'certainty' in the sense of 'mathematical accuracy,' will often be impossible to achieve. Uncertainty can arise in such cases due to the fact that the 'but for' position is often based upon an 'estimated'/'hypothetical' situation.

[8] As, for example, where a 'global'/cumulative financial loss is the result of more than 1 causative factor: Crosby (J) & Sons Ltd v Portland Urban District Council (6.17); Penvidic Contracting Co v International Nickel Co of Canada (6.14); Government of Ceylon v Chandris (6.21-23).

[9] If actual cost records are not available or if the situation is so complex that cost records would not necessarily lead to greater accuracy the claimant can appoint an expert witness to give an opinion as to the financial effects of the breach. The judge/arbitrator might accept the evidence, such as in Penvidic Contracting Co v International Nickel Co of Canada (6.14), alternatively the tribunal could make its own assessment, perhaps taking into account any technical data which the experts considered to be relevant: Thompson and others v Smiths Shiprepairers (North Shields) Ltd (6.24-26).

[10] Chaplin v Hicks (6.10); Ratcliffe v Evans (6.11-12); Penvidic Contracting Co v International Nickel Co of Canada/Wood v Grand Valley Ry Co (6.14); Government of Ceylon v Chandris (6.21-23); Thompson and others v Smiths Shiprepairers (North Shields) Ltd (6.24-26).

injury/harm has occurred.[11] If, for whatever reason, it would be senseless/pedantic[12] to search for greater certainty/accuracy, damages will be awarded "however rough and ready the result" of the assessment[13]/even if the assessment is "a matter of guesswork."[14] So far as assessment of damages is concerned, the overriding principle is that:

".....the court should make the best estimate which it can, in the light of the evidence,.."[15]

6.9 In some situations the only facts available may be the nature

---

[11] It is important to distinguish a situation in which it is 'impossible to assess' damages (meaning 'impossible to assess with certainty/accuracy') and a situation in which it is 'impossible to say whether a factor has caused any harm/injury.' In the former situation a 'best estimate' should be made even if the amount is a matter of guesswork (6.8). In the latter, whichever party is asserting has failed to discharge the burden of proof. The point is illustrated by the case of Government of Ceylon v Chandris (6.21-23) and by Thompson and others v Smiths Shiprepairers (North Shields) Ltd (6.24-26).

[12] Thompson and others v Smiths Shiprepairers (North Shields) Ltd (6.24-26)/Ratcliffe v Evans (6.11-12).

[13] Mustill J in Thompson and others v Smiths Shiprepairers (North Shields) Ltd at (6.24-26).

[14] Chaplin v Hicks (6.10); Penvidic Contracting Co v International Nickel Co of Canada/Wood v Grand Valley Ry Co (6.14); Government of Ceylon v Chandris (6.21-23). An appeal against an assessment of damages will only be allowed in limited circumstances (6.27-28).

[15] Chaplin v Hicks (6.10); Biggin and Co Ltd and Another v Permanite Ltd (6.13); Penvidic Contracting Co v International Nickel Co of Canada/Wood v Grand Valley Ry Co (6.14); Thompson and others v Smiths Shiprepairers (North Shields) Ltd (6.24-26). The quotation is from Mustill J in Thompson at p910 (6.25).

of the breach and the fact/inference, or 'presumption' in some cases,[16] that some harm has occurred. Applying the principle in paragraph 6.8, this is sufficient information from which to make an assessment. The term 'nominal' damages is sometimes used to describe the award/claimant's entitlement in such circumstances.[17] Awards in such cases are, however, made with some 'reference to reality or fact'/'with reasons' albeit to a varied extent. The amount of the award may depend upon the nature of the breach, the level of awards in similar cases and the other circumstances of the case. In all cases it is necessary to make the best estimate of the monetary value of the harm done.

In some cases the claimant has been held entitled to a 'token' award of say £5, where an inference or a presumption of some harm/injury cannot be made, that is where the claimant fails to discharge the burden of proof. Such an award is also referred to as 'nominal' damages and when used in this context it leads to the creation of a further category of damages, namely 'substantial' damages. It is therefore said that to be entitled to 'substantial' damages, the claimant must prove that he has suffered 'actual' damage/harm. It is wrong however to create such special 'categories of damages' not

---

[16] When a wrong is said to be actionable 'per se,' it means that it is actionable 'as of right/without proof of damage.' Examples include the torts of trespass and some forms of defamation. In some cases, such as 'malicious falsehood' the presumption of harm in favour of the claimant is at least in part due to the fact that actual harm/damage would otherwise be difficult for the claimant to prove.

[17] 'Nominal' damages are said to be recoverable, for example, in cases of trespass, malicious falsehood, breach of covenant, inability to show good title (sale of land). 'Nominal' is an ambiguous term with several meanings, including: merely named, stated, or expressed, without reference to reality or fact; (of fee etc) small, insignificant; minimal symbolic, token.

least due to the fact that it is inconsistent with the underlying principle (1.2) which requires that there should be some damage/harm before an entitlement to compensation arises. In Shevill and others v Presse Alliance SA,[18] Lord Jauncey said that:

> "An award of even nominal damages is recognition of some harm having been suffered by the plaintiff."

d. Particular problems

6.10 'Lost opportunity' claims.[19] In Chaplin v Hicks,[20] the claimant was one of 50 ladies selected for interview in respect of 12 contracts available to theatre actresses. She was unable to attend on the only day fixed for interview and sought damages in respect of the 'lost opportunity' of being selected for employment. It was held that she had not been afforded a reasonable opportunity of presenting herself for selection and damages were assessed at £100. On appeal Vaughan Williams LJ said (at p792) that:

> ".... In such a case[21] the jury must do the best they can, and it may be that the amount of their verdict will really be a matter of guesswork. But the fact that

---

[18] [1996] 3 All ER 929, HL.

[19] Illustrated by Victoria Laundry (Windsor) Ltd v Newman Industries LTD (5.8).

[20] [1911] 2 KB 786 (CA).

[21] His Lordship was considering a situation involving breach of a contract for delivery of goods where there is no market for the goods at the relevant time.

damages cannot be assessed with certainty does not relieve the wrongdoer of the necessity of paying damages for his breach of contract."

At p795 Fletcher Moulton LJ stated that:

"I think that, where it is clear that there has been actual loss resulting from the breach of contract, which it is difficult to estimate in money, it is for the jury to do their best to estimate; it is not necessary that there should be an absolute measure of damages in each case. ....Where by a contract a man has a right to belong to a limited class of competitors, he is possessed of something of value, and it is the duty of the jury to estimate the pecuniary value of that advantage taken from him. ...They [the jury] must of course give effect to the consideration that the plaintiff's chance is only one out of four and that they cannot tell whether she would have ultimately proved to be the winner. But having considered all this they may well think that it is of considerable pecuniary value to have got into so small a class, and they must assess the damages accordingly."

6.11 Ratcliffe v Evans[22] concerned an action for loss of business suffered as a result of a false and malicious statement printed in a newspaper. At trial the claimant "proved a general loss of business since the publication" but was unable to identify loss of specific customers influenced by the statement. The wrongdoer asserted that actual losses should be particularised (6.5) and that the claim should therefore fail. Damages of £120 were awarded. On appeal the question was whether such

---

[22] Ratcliffe v Evans [1892] 2 QB 524 (CA).

'general' evidence of damage was admissible and sufficient. At pp531 and 532 Bowen LJ stated that:

"....."damages in the 'per quod,' [ie actual damage] where the 'per quod' is the gist of the action, should be shewn certainly and specially," But such a doctrine as this was always subject to the qualification of good sense and justice. Cases may here, as before, occur where a general loss of custom is the natural and direct result of the slander, and where it is not possible to specify particular instances of the loss........ ...The necessity of alleging and proving actual temporal loss with certainty and precision in all cases of the sort has been insisted upon for centuries..... But it is ancient and established rule of pleading that the question of generality of pleading must depend on the general subject matter..... In all actions accordingly on the case where the damage actually done is the gist of the action, the character of the acts themselves which produce the damage, and the circumstances under which these acts are done, must regulate the degree of certainty and particularity with which the damage done ought to be stated and proved. As much certainty and particularity must be insisted on, both in pleading and proof of damage, as is reasonable, having regard to the circumstances and to the nature of the acts themselves by which the damage is done.[23] To insist upon less would be to relax old and intelligible principles. To insist upon more would be the vainest pedantry."

---

[23] In addition, "the degree of accuracy demanded should be commensurate with the degree of accuracy possible:" Mustill J in Thompson and others v Smiths Shiprepairers (North Shields) Ltd (6.24-26).

6.12 Taking a slightly different approach it could be said that the first issue in the Ratcliffe case was whether the claimants had, on the balance of probabilities, proved that the statement had caused *any* 'loss of business.' This burden may have been discharged, for example, by giving uncontradicted oral evidence to the effect that there had been a downturn in business.[24] Had the matter been considered in this way Bowen LJ might have concluded that "to insist upon more would be to forget that the standard of proof is the balance of probabilities."

The second issue would have been 'how much?' As specific losses had not been particularised/given it was necessary to make the 'best estimate' in the light of the evidence. The exact amount would perhaps have depended on the seriousness of the libel, the nature and turnover of the business and the other circumstances of the case.

6.13 Evidential problems/cost records not available. The fact that 'better' evidence (with accuracy of assessment in mind) might have been adduced in support of the claim for damages does not mean that an assessment should not be made. In Biggin and Co Ltd and Another v Permanite Ltd[25] Devlin J said that:

> "Where precise evidence is obtainable, the court naturally expects to have it, [but] where it is not, the

---

[24] The report of the case does not state precisely how the burden was discharged.

[25] [1950] 2 All ER 859 at 870.

court must do the best it can."[26]

The credibility or weight to be attached to particular evidence is however something which is bound to affect the amount of the award (6.4). In Garton v Hunter,[27] Lord Denning MR said that:

"Nowadays we do not confine ourselves to the best evidence. We admit all relevant evidence. The goodness or badness of it goes only to weight, and not to admissibility."

6.14 If records of actual costs or other matters are unavailable, the claimant may adduce expert evidence as to the amount of loss/effect of the breach.[28] In Penvidic Contracting Co v International Nickel Co of Canada[29] a railroad contractor had undertaken to carry out track laying and surface ballasting to a 47.5 mile long railroad in Manitoba. The employer was in breach of its implied obligation 'to facilitate the work' in a number of respects including failure to provide the necessary

---

[26] See also Mustill J in Thompson and others v Smiths Shiprepairers (North Shields) Ltd (6.24-26). In that case the claimant's were to be given the benefit of any doubt as to the amount recoverable due to the fact that the respondent/employer had failed to take contemporaneous audiograms.

[27] [1969] 2 QB 37; [1969] 1 All ER 451, CA

[28] This is the case whatever the reason for difficulty of assessment (6.7 and 6.8).

[29] (1975) 53 DLR (3d) 748 Can Sup Ct.

rail link to an existing railway for plant access.[30] This factor alone resulted in revision to the whole method of construction whereby the contractor was required to commence work at a half way point and work in two directions. In the first instance, the contractor revalued the work[31] claiming an additional 25c per ton on the contractual rate for top ballasting in compensation. This was based upon the difference between the contractual rate per ton of ballast and the rate which he would have demanded had he foreseen the adverse conditions caused by the failure to provide the rail link.[32] At trial the contractor, due to having insufficient cost data, claimed damages for breach of the implied term assessed on the same basis as the revaluation of the work. The claim for damages was successful and in the Supreme Court of Canada Spence J said (at p755) that:

> "In an ordinary case, the plaintiff in an action for damages for such breaches of contract would prove the additional costs which it incurred. As Wilson J points

---

[30] In addition the contractor "met with many frustrations in the completion of its contract." The other breaches by the employer included failure by its other contractors to complete the sub-base for the road, failure to obtain access under electricity pylons and failure to obtain leave to cross a highway. These factors caused months of delay in completion of the contract.

[31] The revaluation was made on the basis of a 'variation,' alternatively a 'substituted contract' rather than breach of an implied term.

[32] This approach would give effect to terms such as 'fair valuation' and 'reasonable rates' which are used, for example, in JCT and ICE standard forms of building/engineering contracts: see Crosby (J) & Sons Ltd v Portland Urban District Council (6.17). 'Repricing'/'revaluation' is also the method adopted for the recovery of 'compensation' under the Engineering and Construction Contract.

out in his reasons for judgement, despite the length of the trial, "...the evidence was not as helpful as one would have expected and more records giving more particulars of when and where different types of work were being done would have been very useful." Under these circumstances, the plaintiff chose to put its claim for this extra ballasting on the basis of a claim for an additional sum per ton. That is the fashion in which it had attempted to have the respondent agree to pay extra compensation. That such an attempt ended in failure does not prevent the award of damages using the same measure as had been used in the vain attempt to obtain extra compensation.

The learned trial judge expressly accepted the evidence of ...an independent witness giving evidence for the plaintiff, who was asked this question:
Q: And as a person who has advised in bidding on these jobs, what do you think of the figure of 60c a ton for laying ballast by the method that he was, in the main, obliged to use?
A: Reasonable"[33]

On the issue as to whether the trial judge was correct to allow an assessment of damages on the basis of a 'revaluation' of work Spence J referred to a number of authorities including Wood v Grand Valley R. Co.[34] In that case Davies J had said as follows in applying the underlying principle (6.8) laid down in Chaplin v Hicks (6.10):

---

[33] The expert also gave his opinion in relation to the originally proposed track laying method (p756).

[34] (1913) 16 DLR 361.

"It was clearly impossible under the facts of that case to estimate with anything approaching mathematical accuracy the damages sustained by the plaintiffs, but it seems to me to be clearly laid down there by the learned Judges that such an impossibility cannot "relieve the wrongdoer of the necessity of paying damages for his breach of contract" and that on the other hand the tribunal to estimate them whether jury or Judge must under such circumstances do "the best it can" and its conclusion will not be set aside even if *"the amount of the verdict is a matter of guess work.""* (Emphasis added by Spence J).

Spence J then said (at p757) that:

"I can see no objection whatsoever to the learned trial Judge using the method suggested by the plaintiff of assessing the damages in the form of additional compensation per ton rather than attempting to reach it by ascertaining items of expense from records which, by the very nature of the contract, had to be fragmentary and probably mere estimations."[35]

6.15 Global claims. A 'global'/'rolled up' claim is made where the injured party seeks to recover a cumulative/global loss alleging that the loss was caused by (the cumulative effect of) two or more breaches (figure 6.1). This approach is appropriate, and a 'global' award can be made, if the amount of damage attributable to each breach cannot in reality be

---

[35] 'Actual costs records' might therefore have made no difference to the method of assessment.

separated[36] or if no greater degree of accuracy would be achieved by allocating damage and/or delay to the various causative factors.[37]

6.16 'Global' loss and 'one and indivisible' loss distinguished. The distinction between a 'global'/'cumulative' loss situation (figure 6.1) and a 'one and indivisible' loss situation (figure 2.7) is considered at 2.22.

Fig 6.1: Is it necessary to allocate damage to each breach or can a 'global' assessment be made?

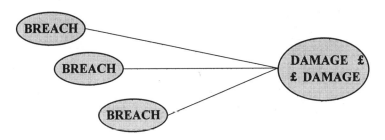

6.17 Crosby (J) & Sons Ltd v Portland Urban District Council[38] was concerned with a dispute arising from a contract for the construction of a pipeline under ICE standard from of contract 4th edition. Variations were instructed in respect of the line of the pipe, the method of working and in respect of significant

---

[36] Crosby (J) & Sons Ltd v Portland Urban District Council (6.17); London Borough of Merton v Stanley Hugh Leach Ltd (6.18).

[37] Thompson and others v Smiths Shiprepairers (North Shields) Ltd (6.24-26).

[38] (1967) 5 BLR 121, QBD.

amounts of additional work. There was also an element of contractor's default and neutral events.

Fig 6.2: Crosby v Portland UDC

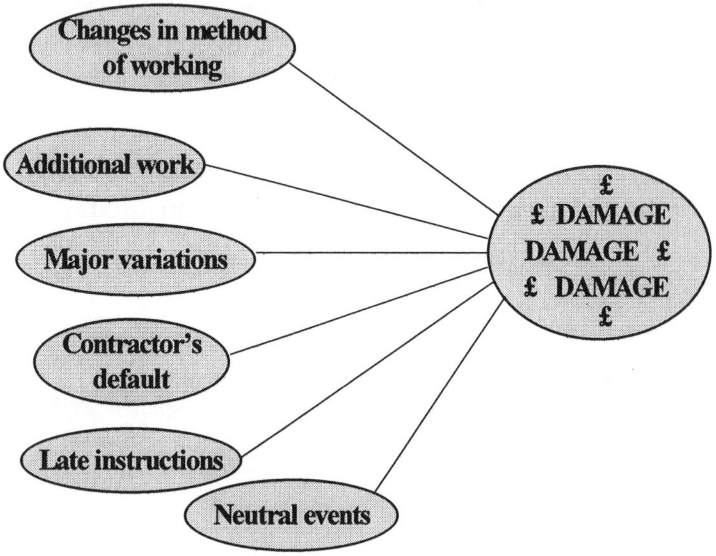

The arbitrator ordered that amounts attributable to certain items should be assessed by way of varied rates.[39] In respect of the balance, the contractor submitted a general, 'global,' claim for delay and disorganisation. The arbitrator held that 31 weeks of the 46 week delay was due to the various matters for

---

[39] The 'revaluation' approach is generally the approach which should be taken in the first instance under most standard forms of construction contract (6.14). Assigning a 'value' to the change/breach was the approach taken in Penvidic Contracting Co v International Nickel Co of Canada (6.14) and in Thompson and others v Smiths Shiprepairers (North Shields) Ltd (6.24-26).

which the employer was responsible and that part of the disorganisation of labour cost was also attributable to these matters. He held that it was "impracticable if not impossible" to allocate parts of the 'rolled up' award to any one of the causative factors in isolation. As to whether the arbitrator's approach was correct, Donaldson J said (at p136) that:

> "I can see no reason why he should not recognise the realities of the situation and make individual awards in respect of those parts of individual items of the claim which can be dealt with in isolation and a supplementary award in respect of the remainder of these claims as a composite whole. This is what the arbitrator has done...."

6.18 The issue as to whether a 'global' assessment could be made also arose in the case of London Borough of Merton v Stanley Hugh Leach Ltd.[40] In that case the contract (JCT 63 Standard Form of Building Contract) expressly required that delay and damage should be allocated to each causative factor. As to whether this was a condition precedent to recovery, Vinelott J said that:

> "If ... it is impracticable to disentangle or disintegrate the part directly attributable to each head of claim, then ....the architect must ascertain the global loss directly attributable to the two causes. ...To this extent the law supplements the contractual machinery which no longer works in the way in which it was intended to work so as to ensure that the contractor is not unfairly deprived of the benefit which the parties clearly intend

---

[40] (1985) 32 BLR 51.

he should have."[41]

e. Apportionment of loss/damage

6.19 Apportionment of loss/damage. Apportionment of damage
is necessary if part of the total/cumulative loss is due to the
claimant's own fault or some other cause for which the
wrongdoer is not responsible (figure 6.3).
Assessment/apportionment is made by making the best
estimate in the light of the evidence of the amount attributable
to each or either cause (6.8).

**Fig 6.3: Is it permissible to apportion loss/damage
where the injured party is partly responsible for the
global loss?**

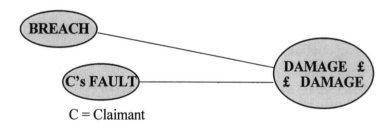

C = Claimant

**6.20 Distinction between 'apportionment of damage' and
'apportionment of liability.'[42]** Apportionment of damage
involves an assessment of the 'relative effect' of each

---

[41] (1985) 32 BLR 51 at pp102-103, applying the decision in Crosby (J) &
Sons Ltd v Portland Urban District Council (6.17).

[42] The distinction is also considered at 3.3.

causative factor.[43] Apportionment of liability (chapter 3) is concerned with an assessment of the 'relative fault/blameworthiness' of the parties (3.2). In each case the purpose of the exercise is the same, that is, to assess the extent of the wrongdoer's liability for the total loss incurred.[44]

6.21 In Government of Ceylon v Chandris[45] the Government of Ceylon (the claimant/charterers) brought an action against Chandris (the owner/respondent) for breach of a contract for the carriage of a cargo of rice. The rice was shipped in bags and in good condition. On arrival some of the bags were found to contain 'sweat' damaged rice[46] and many bags had been torn and were empty. As regards the bags containing sweat damaged rice, the umpire stated as follows (p52):

> "In so far as they are questions of fact I find, and in so far as they are questions of law hold: ... 4. That the damage to the 2,406 bags of rice was caused by sweat (condensation) ..... and seawater: that the majority of the damage was caused by sweat but that it was impossible upon the evidence to say how much of the

---

[43] Note, for example, the reference to 'the majority of the damage' at paragraph 4 of the award in Government of Ceylon v Chandris (6.21-23) and the comments by Mustill J in his conclusions in Thompson and others v Smiths Shiprepairers (North Shields) Ltd (6.24-26).

[44] The distinction is due to the fact that in the former situation the loss is 'global'/cumulative in nature whereas in the latter the loss is 'one and indivisible' (2.22).

[45] [1965] 3 All ER 48

[46] The loss consisted of the 'diminution in value' of the rice. The reduction in value was due to the fact that it had become unfit for human consumption [1965] 3 All ER 48 at 51-52.

damage was attributable to each cause. 5. That the vessel was inadequately fitted for the carriage of the cargo of rice in that the holds were neither fitted with closely spaced cargo battens nor were they dunnaged with bamboo: that this deficiency prevented the free circulation of air in the holds and was one of the causes of sweating; that this deficiency also resulted in damage to the bags of rice in that in the absence of closely spaced cargo battens or bamboos sweat on the sides and bulkheads of the holds came in contact with the bags. 6. Sweating was also caused by the necessary restriction of ventilation during the voyage and by the long duration of the voyage[47] and that some damage to the bags of rice would have resulted even had the vessel been adequately fitted. 7. That it was impossible to say what proportion of the damage was caused by the matters referred to in the immediately preceding two sub-paragraphs … 10. That the owner failed to establish what proportion of the damage was caused by events for which by the charterparty she was not liable.[48] 11. That the owner is liable to the charterers in respect of the 2,406 bags of rice delivered damaged at Colombo."

6.22 Having concluded that several factors were causative of *some* damage/harm (paragraphs 4 and 6 of the award) then,

---

[47] The "long duration of the voyage" is a reference to a 120 day delay caused by the claimant's own fault.

[48] "The argument turned in the main on questions relating to the burden of proof:" Mocatta J at p51.

applying the underlying principle (6.8),[49] the arbitrator was incorrect, as a matter of law, in deciding (at paragraphs 4 and 7) that it was impossible to apportion the damage.[50] At p56-57 Mocatta J said that:

"... when some part of a claimant's goods has undoubtedly been damaged by the carrier's breach of contract and some by the claimant's own breach of contract, the tribunal should be slow to award only nominal damages because of the paucity of primary facts from which the quantum of damages due to the claimant's own breach can be inferred.[51] Juries, arbitrators, judges, and even the Court of Appeal (see, for example, *Silver v Ocean Steamship Co Ltd* per Scrutton LJ ([1929] All ER Rep 611; [1930] 1 KB 416 at p 429)) have not infrequently to make what may in truth be little more than informed guesses at the quantum of damages by drawing inferences from the primary facts proved before them. ....., the burden of proof rests on the claimants to prove the damages to which they are entitled over and above nominal

---

[49] That is, that the tribunal "should make the best estimate which it can, in the light of the evidence."

[50] He presumably meant 'impossible to assess with certainty/accuracy' (6.8). See also Mustill J in Thompson and others v Smiths Shiprepairers (North Shields) Ltd (6.24-26) at 909: "The fact that precise quantification is impossible ...."

[51] 'Nominal damages' is an ambiguous term (6.9). The overriding principle is that the tribunal should make the best estimate in the light of the evidence even if this means making an informed guess (6.8). The outcome could therefore be a 50/50 apportionment or any other apportionment depending on the umpire's view as to the 'relative effect' of each causative factor.

damages.[52] The umpire should also remember that he is entitled, like any tribunal, to draw inferences from primary facts. Only if, after the most careful consideration of the primary facts proved, he finds it impossible to draw any fair inference as to the quantity of damage caused by the claimants' breach or breaches of contract or by the respondent's breach of contract, should he finally fall back on the law as to the burden of proof as indicated above."[53]

6.23 On the basis of the umpire's findings a number of apportionments/sub-apportionments would have been necessary. As to responsibility for the various causative factors, the seawater damage (paragraph 4) and inadequate fitting of the vessel (paragraph 5) were the responsibility of the owner.[54] The first and third causes in paragraph 6 would appear to have been matters which were the fault of neither party[55] and 'the long duration of the voyage' was due to the charterer's default in detaining the vessel for 120 days over

---

[52] This could be interpreted as meaning that 'if the claimant fails to prove *any* loss/injury then he is only entitled to a 'nominal' (in the sense of a 'token') amount of damages.' Such an interpretation would however be inaccurate (6.9).

[53] If a party proves that a breach by the other party was a cause of *some* harm/injury then that is sufficient to discharge the burden of proof. Thereafter the tribunal should make the best estimate as to the amount thereof (6.8 and 6.19). The findings at paragraphs 10 and 11 of the award must, therefore, be incorrect.

[54] The seawater damage was caused by a lack of tarpaulins (owner's breach): [1965] 3 All ER 48 at 51.

[55] The charterer would perhaps be taken to have assumed the risk in respect of this type of loss on entering into the contract.

the permitted lay time.

On the assumption that damage to the rice was proportional to the duration of the voyage[56] then the first calculation would involve an apportionment of the total damage (A) to arrive at amounts in respect of the initial damage (B) and the further damage caused as a result of the period of delay (C).[57] Thereafter further 'sub-apportionments' would have to be made in respect of amounts (B) and (C) as illustrated by figure 6.4.

Fig 6.4: Government of Ceylon v Chandris

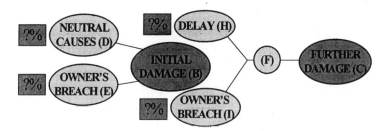

As regards the initial damage (B) a deduction would have to be made in respect of neutral causes/damage which was the fault of neither party (D).[58] It would not be necessary to make

---

[56] That is, in the absence of technical evidence to the contrary/in order to simplify matters.

[57] The question which might be asked is: 'how much additional sweat damage/depreciation in value was caused during the period of delay?' A very similar issue arose in Thompson and others v Smiths Shiprepairers (North Shields) Ltd (6.24-26).

[58] Since the neutral causes and the owner's breach would each have been causes of damage (when considered in isolation) the initial damage (B) could not have been 'one and indivisible' (2.22). Since the owner's breach

a 'sub-apportionment' of the balance (E) as both causes at paragraph 4 of the award were (prior to any delay) the responsibility of the owner. As to the further damage (C) any further effect of the 'neutral' factors could first be isolated (F).[59] The remaining damage during the period of delay (G), which is not shown in figure 6.4, would be a 'one and indivisible' loss caused by the combined effect of the delay (H) and the continuing effect of the owner's breach in not providing an adequately fitted vessel (I). This gives rise to a figure 2.8 situation (2.23)[60] and it would therefore have been necessary to consider whether apportionment of liability (chapter 3) was appropriate.

6.24 An issue of apportionment of loss/damage arose in Thompson and others v Smiths Shiprepairers (North Shields) Ltd.[61] The case concerned an action by employees for damages for progressive hearing impairment sustained as a result of excessive noise in the workplace. The damage was sustained over a period stretching from the 1940s (or earlier) to the 1970s. Mustill J held that 1963 was the date at which the

---

would have caused 'further' rather than the 'same' sweat damage the loss is a global/cumulative one (figure 6.1) rather than one involving concurrent causes of the same damage (figure 2.4).

[59] If 'additional' loss of this type had been incurred as a 'consequence' of the extension to the duration of the voyage then the charterer and the owner would have been liable in respect thereof (4.18-19) in proportion to their responsibility for the remaining loss (G) (not shown).

[60] The issue considered in chapter 4, as to whether the chain of causation had been broken, would not apply since the 'delay' was not a 'consequence' of a breach of duty, in this case the inadequate fitting of the vessel. Otherwise the case is similar to The Calliope (4.9/figure4.4).

[61] [1984] 1 All ER 881, QBD.

employers ought to have provided protection against noise and that the damage which occurred thereafter, the 'additional detriment,' consisted of an acceleration of progress towards disability and handicap. It followed that from 1963 the employer should have taken audiograms in order to monitor hearing loss. They had failed to do this, however, and each party adduced complex expert evidence as to how the 'amount of hearing loss' at 1963 should be assessed.[62] As to the degree of accuracy/certainty required in the making of the assessment/apportionment Mustill J said (at p906) that:

"How precise must this division be, before it can found an apportionment in law? What happens if the apportionment is insufficiently precise?[63] To the latter question, general principle supplies only a guarded answer.[64] In strict logic, the plaintiff should fail for want of proof that the breach has caused the damage.[65] Yet this seems *too* strict, for the plaintiff has proved some loss;[66] perhaps it should all be attributed to the

---

[62] This evidence included a variety of tables, graphs and calculations and extracts from literature and articles from journals.

[63] In other words, 'what degree of certainty/accuracy is required?'

[64] The overriding statement of principle, namely that the court should make the best estimate which it can in the light of the evidence (p910) answers both of these questions.

[65] By this it is meant 'caused a specific/certain amount of damage' - it is not a reference to the issue of causation (chapter 2).

[66] It would be "too strict" to award nothing. Hence the court should make the best estimate it can, even if the award is a matter of guesswork. (6.8).

fault, simply as a matter of policy.[67] The answer to the
first question seems less difficult. The degree of
accuracy demanded should be commensurate with the
degree of accuracy possible, in the light of existing
knowledge, and with the degree of accuracy involved
in the remainder of the exercise which leads to the
computation of damages.[68] It is senseless to demand the
utmost accuracy at one stage of a calculation, which
involves the broadest assumptions at another stage, and
the application of conventional measures of recovery at
yet another. I return to this point later."

6.25 Prior to reaching his conclusions on the issues of law his
Lordship considered whether as a matter of principle the
claimants ought to have been allowed recovery in full due to
the employer's failure to take audiograms. At (at p909-910) he
said that:

"[the plaintiffs submit that] The reason why precise
quantification is impossible lies in the very fact that the
employers had failed to protect their workmen by
taking audiograms at the proper time. In such
circumstances, fairness demands that the plaintiffs
should be entitled to recover their loss in full.
Whilst I sympathise with this contention, I cannot
accept it. The defendants as well as the plaintiffs are
entitled to a just result. If we know (and we do know,
for by the end of the case it was no longer seriously in

---

[67] This scenario is rejected in the next paragraph.

[68] The degree of accuracy possible may also depend on the availability of
evidence. The effect of the overriding principle (6.8), referred to at p910
of the judgment, is that no particular degree of accuracy is required.

dispute) that a substantial part of the impairment took place before the defendants were in breach, why in fairness should they be made to pay for it? The fact that precise quantification is impossible[69] should not alter the position. The whole exercise of assessing damages is shot through with imprecision.[70] Even the measurements of the plaintiffs' hearing loss contain a substantial margin of error. The use of an average involves an over-simplification, and the choice of frequencies for the average materially affects the apparent outcome of the measurements. The translation of impairment into disability is arbitrary. The translation of disability into handicap requires a purely judgmental assessment by the court of the effect which the disability has had on the circumstances of the individual plaintiff. The last stage of the process, which requires the assessed handicap to be turned into an award of damages, again requires the court, as a matter of judgment, to place the plaintiff at the correct point on a scale of possible monetary awards, accommodating all ranges of deafness from the very worst to the very least, a scale which is itself arbitrary by its very nature.

Thus, whatever the position might be if the court were to find itself unable to make any findings at all on

---

[69] Impossible 'due to unavailability of evidence/contemporaneous records.'

[70] Even if contemporaneous evidence had been available the assessment process was, due to 'scientific complexity,' shot through with imprecision. The same point is made in Penvidic Contracting Co v International Nickel Co of Canada (6.14).

the issue of causation[71] and was accordingly being faced with a choice between awarding for the defendants in full, or for the plaintiff in full, or on some wholly arbitrary basis such as an award of 50%, I see no reason why the present impossibility of making a precise apportionment of impairment and disability in terms of time, should in justice lead to the result that the defendants are adjudged liable to pay in full, when it is known that only part of the damage was their fault. What justice does demand, to my mind, is that **the court should make the best estimate which it can, in the light of the evidence,**[72] making the fullest allowances in favour of the plaintiffs for the uncertainties known to be involved in any apportionment.[73] In the end, notwithstanding all the care lavished on it by the scientists and by counsel I believe that this has to be regarded as a jury question,[74] and I propose to approach it as such."

6.26 Making the 'best estimate' inevitably involves making a choice between (or adopting a combination of) different potential methods of assessment. In the Thompson case Mustill J concluded (at p915) as follows:

---

[71] This is a reference back to the second question at 906, that is 'what if it is impossible to say how much damage was caused by the breach?'

[72] In the present case it was the 'albeit incomplete evidence.' See also Devlin J in Biggin and Co Ltd and Another v Permanite Ltd (6.13).

[73] This part of the reasoning stems from the fact that the defendants "had failed to protect their workmen by taking audiograms at the proper time..." (909h).

[74] Amount/quantum is a question of fact (6.2).

"Conclusions

I now proceed at last to draw together these conclusions of law and fact.

First, I must consider whether the apportionment exercise is legitimate at all, or whether the attempt to ascertain the handicap attributable to that part of each plaintiff's employment, which lay between periods where the defendants were not in fault (for want of knowledge) and were not in fault again (because they supplied the requisite protection) would involve such a blind guess that it should not be attempted, but should rather yield to a presumption that all the loss was caused whilst the defendants were in breach. It will, I believe, have already become apparent that in my judgment the exercise should not be rejected. The undeniable imperfections and inaccuracies of the process need no further emphasis. I acknowledge them all. Nevertheless, a clear picture emerges. To my mind it is absolutely plain that (i) for all plaintiffs, the greater part of the damage at the upper frequencies was done before the breach began, (ii) the loss of the lower frequencies at this time was less, but still really substantial, and (iii) the handicap attributable to the breach was rather greater than the hearing loss curves and tables would suggest, particularly in the case of the group A plaintiffs, whose impairment was already serious enough for any further impairment to be important. I believe that justice can properly be served by giving effect to these findings, however rough and ready the result.

Next, it must be decided how the process should be carried out. One possibility is to assign to each plaintiff the figure which would have been awarded as damages if the whole of the hearing loss had been attributable to the defendants' breach, and then to apply a fraction or percentage representing the court's view of the part which was in fact so attributable. I believe that this is an entirely proper approach where the disability proceeds by clearly identifiable stages, and where the damages appropriate to stage A may be derived by subtracting from the notional total recovery, the damages attaching to stage B. I believe, however, that this may be misleading in a case such as the present, as it gives to the calculation a spurious air of accuracy and might suggest that the chosen percentages are based directly on the defendants' computer print-outs, or similar materials.

In my judgment it is better to go straight to the heart of the problem, by saying that when the breaches began the plaintiffs were persons whose hearing impairments might (in some cases) have caused some unacknowledged disability, but little or no handicap, that these plaintiffs would, as the effects of age progressed, have found themselves becoming subject to patent disability and handicap, that at the time of the breach they were already in a condition where any further exposure to noise would accelerate their progress towards disability and handicap, and that the further exposure during the period of breach did have just this effect. In blunter terms, the plaintiffs were people who in 1963 were already going to be hard of hearing in later life, and the breach merely served to accelerate and enhance the progress. A monetary value should then be directly assigned to this additional detriment. Finally, an eye should be cast on the general level of damages appropriate where liability is established for the whole of the hearing loss, to make sure that the sums awarded for a part of the impairment are not seriously out of proportion.[75] ...

...Treating the matter as a jury question and giving no further reasons beyond saying that I have borne in mind (a) the general configuration of the median curves of the NPL tables, (b) the fact that the effect in terms of disability and hardship of losing a given number of decibels depends on how many have already been lost, and (c) the manifold uncertainties affecting the process of quantification, I make the following awards:....."

f. Appeals

6.27 The courts are reluctant to interfere with another tribunal's assessment of damages. In Davies and Another v Powell Duffryn Associated Collieries Ltd[76] Lord Wright said (at 664-665) that:

"No doubt an appellate court is always reluctant to interfere with a finding of the trial judge on any question of fact, but it is particularly reluctant to interfere with a finding on damages. Such a finding differs from an ordinary finding of fact in that it is generally much more a matter of speculation and estimate. No doubt this statement is truer in respect of some cases than of others. The damages in some cases

---

[75] [1984] 1 All ER 881 at 915h. A similar approach was taken in the Penvidic case (6.14), that is an assessment of the 'value' of the breaches/changes was made. In that case too, no doubt, a cross-reference would have been made to the total amount of the project costs to ensure that the assessed value was not 'seriously out of proportion.'

[76] [1942] 1 All ER 657, HL

may be objective and depend on definite facts and established rules of law, as, for instance, in general damages for breach of contract for the sale of goods. In these cases the finding as to amount of damages differs little from any other finding of fact, and can equally be reviewed if there is error in law or in fact. At the other end of the scale would come damages for pain and suffering or wrongs such as slander. These latter cases are almost entirely matter of impression and of common sense, and are only subject to review in very special cases. There is an obvious difference between cases tried with a jury and cases tried by a judge alone. Where the verdict is that of a jury, it will only be set aside if the appellate court is satisfied that the verdict on damages is such that it is out of all proportion to the circumstances of the case (Mechanical & General Inventions Co v Austin). Where, however, the award is that of the judge alone, the appeal is by way of rehearing on damages as on all other issues, but as there is generally so much room for individual choice so that the assessment of damages is more like an exercise of discretion than an ordinary act of decision, the appellate court is particularly slow to reverse the trial judge on a question of the amount of damages. It is difficult to lay down any precise rule which will cover all cases, but a good general guide is given by Greer LJ, in Flint v Lovell, at p 360. In effect, the court, before it interferes with an award of damages, should be satisfied that the judge has acted upon a wrong principle of law, or has misapprehended the facts, or has for these or other reasons made a wholly erroneous estimate of the damage suffered. It is not enough that there is a balance of opinion or preference. The scale must go down heavily against the figure attacked if the appellate court is to interfere, whether on the ground of excess or insufficiency."

6.28 The decision in the Davies case was followed in Dingle v Associated Newspapers Ltd and Others.[77] In that case Sellers LJ stated (at 908-909) that:

"We were properly referred to what was said by Lord Wright in Davies v Powell Duffryn Associated Collieries Ltd (No 2) and by Viscount Simon in Nance v British Columbia Electric Ry Co Ltd, for direction by which an appellate court should be guided in reviewing damages. If the damages were assessed on a wrong basis at least in part, as I with every respect have had to conclude, then there is no doubt that they call for re-assessment."

[77] [1961] 1 All ER 897.

INDEX